Hiring Great People

Hiring Great People

Kevin C. Klinvex
Matthew S. O'Connell
Christopher P. Klinvex

McGraw-Hill

New York San Francisco Washington, D.C. Auckland Bogotá
Caracas Lisbon London Madrid Mexico City Milan
Montreal New Delhi San Juan Singapore
Sydney Tokyo Toronto

McGraw-Hill

A Division of *The McGraw·Hill Companies*

Copyright © 1999 by The McGraw-Hill Companies, Inc. All rights reserved. Printed in the United States of America. Except as permitted under the United States Copyright Act of 1976, no part of this publication may be reproduced or distributed in any form or by any means, or stored in a database or retrieval system, without the prior written permission of the publisher.

1 2 3 4 5 6 7 8 9 0 DOC/DOC 9 0 3 2 1 0 9 8

ISBN 0-07-071872-5

Library of Congress Cataloging-in-Publication Data

Klinvex, Kevin C.
    Hiring great people / Kevin C. Klinvex, Matthew S. O'Connell, Christopher P. Klinvex
      p. cm.
    A Briefcase Book
    ISBN 0-07-071872-5
    1. Employee selection. I. O'Connell, Matthew S. II. Klinvex, Christopher P.
    HF5549.5.S38K59 1999
    658.3/112 21   98041556

This is a CWL Publishing Enterprises Book, *developed and produced for* McGraw-Hill *by* CWL Publishing Enterprises, *John A. Woods, President. For more information, contact CWL Publishing Enterprises, 3010 Irvington Way, Madison, WI 53713-3414, www.execpc.com/cwlpubent. Robert Magnan served as editor. Page layout by Cleveland Publishing Services, Madison, WI. For McGraw-Hill, the sponsoring editor was Catherine Schwent, the publisher was Jeffrey Krames, the editing supervisor was John M. Morriss, and the production supervisor was Suzanne W. B. Rapcavage.*

Printed and bound by R. R. Donnelley & Sons Company

Contents

Preface

"We need to do something different this time around," Sara said with a sigh.

"You're right. Our last round of hiring was a nightmare!" Charlie grumbled.

"Our hiring process used to work really well. People were lining up outside just hoping to get a chance to come to work for us. We had our pick of the cream of the crop," lamented Al.

"What's changed? Why don't we have the applicant appeal like we've had in the past? We are still a great company to work for. I just don't get it!" Charlie was just about at his wit's end.

"Recruiting is definitely a problem, but it's not the only one. Our selection tools aren't working like they used to. Our basic skills test and interview process aren't helping us choose people who are going to succeed here," explained Sara.

"That's right, Sara. All you need to do is take a look around. Let's be honest. Our most recent new hires just aren't cutting the mustard," Charlie added.

Are you experiencing the pains of trying to attract the right people for your jobs and being disappointed with your results? Are you having a hard time identifying which applicants would be most likely to succeed in your jobs? If so, you are not alone.

No matter how big or small your business may be, and regardless of what industry you are in, managers across the country are under pressure to find and keep high-performing employees. Low unemployment, the increasing demand for technical skills, and the need for a multiskilled workforce have presented new challenges to the hiring process. In order to compete in today's global market, companies must have access to cutting-edge information, tools, processes, and ideas that will help them recruit and select people who are capable of making real contributions to their company's future success. That is the objective of this book.

Why Read This Book?

Think of this book as your complete resource guide to hiring. From front to back, this book contains practical information that can save your company time and money in the hiring process. Many of the techniques and tips described can be implemented quickly and without a lot of resource investment; others may require more investment up front, but pay out large dividends in the long term.

Over time, the cost of turnover, poor quality, and low productivity will always be more than the costs of investing in an effective hiring process. Consider the time spent interviewing candidates and training new hires. Now think about other factors that contribute to the cost of making a poor hiring decision, such as advertising, training, decreased productivity, and related administrative duties. The table on the next page shows the average cost of hiring a candidate for a position at an annual salary of $35,000. As you can see in the table, making even one poor hiring decision can be quite costly.

Overview of the Book

In the first chapter, you'll learn the steps you need to take to identify the knowledge, skills, abilities, and motivations that are required for success in your jobs. This chapter serves as the foundation for every other chapter of the book.

Activity	Cost
Advertising Number of Ads x cost per ad: 1 x $1500	$1,500

Training
    3 months salary + benefits (about 30%)
    $8,750 + $2,625
	$11,375

Interviewer Costs
    Number of interviewers x hours per candidate x average
    hourly salary + benefits x number of candidates
    3 x 1 x $30 x 4
	$360

Administrative Costs
    Number of hours x average hourly salary + benefits
    20 x $115
	$300

Lost Opportunities
    Revenue lost from incomplete projects and/or poor
    performance by incompetent employees
	$30,000

Total	**$43,535***

*Candidate travel costs and relocation fees can double or even triple this figure.

In the second chapter, we talk about discrimination and some of the major federal laws affecting the hiring process. While this chapter is not meant to be a thorough review of the law, it does provide a sound rationale for using standard selection procedures similar to the ones we describe in later chapters.

In Chapter 3 you'll learn how to "market" your company in a way that will attract the applicants that you are seeking. In this chapter, we present a variety of advertising and public relations activities that will catch—and keep—the attention of today's most desirable candidates.

In Chapters 4 and 5, you will learn how to use your employment application as a screening tool. We show you how to set up a structured system for screening applications and résumés and determining which applicants should be invited to participate in the next stage in the hiring process.

Chapters 6 and 7 deal with interviews. We first talk about how to avoid some of the most common pitfalls to interviewing, and then you'll learn how to conduct an interview that will help you to better predict success on the job.

In Chapter 8, you will learn how to assess a candidate's motivation to do the job. This is a key area to assess because motivation can sometimes be a better predictor of performance than one's skills and abilities.

Chapter 9 focuses on the use of tests in selection. In this chapter, you'll learn how to choose tests that actually predict how well people will perform once they are hired and on the job.

Chapter 10 provides guidance for conducting background checks. In this chapter, we'll explain why you should do them and how to do them.

Chapters 11 and 12 deal with the final stages of the selection process: making final hiring decisions, negotiating job offers, and orienting new employees. Once you've invested in the activities described in earlier chapters, you will want to make sure that you know what you're doing in these important final stages.

The last chapter covers alternative staffing options. The pros and cons associated with the use of part-time employees, temporary workers, independent contractors, and outsourcing are discussed.

As you can see, this book covers the hiring process from start to finish. We have included the most accurate and up-to-date information that can be applied today to help you select a better workforce for tomorrow. Whether this is the first, or the twenty-first, time that you've been involved in the hiring process, you will benefit from reading this book. We provide all the groundwork for someone who is new to hiring, as well as the most current techniques that can help even experienced managers improve their hiring process.

Special Features

The idea behind the books in the Briefcase Series is to give you practical information written in a friendly person-to-person style. The chapters are short, deal with tactical issues, and include lots of examples. They also feature numerous boxes designed to give you different types of specific information. Here's a description of the boxes you'll find in this book.

 These boxes do just what they say: give you tips and tactics for being smart in making hiring decisions.

 These boxes provide warnings for where things could go wrong when you hire new employees.

 Here you'll find how-to hints to make the hiring process go easier.

 Every subject has its special jargon and terms. These boxes provide definitions of these concepts.

 Want to know how others have done it? Look for these boxes.

 Here you'll find specific procedures you can follow in the hiring process to get good results.

 How can you make sure you won't make a mistake when hiring? You can't, but these boxes will give you practical advice on how to minimize the possibility.

Acknowledgments

Books are always a collaboration. From the time we got the call to write *Hiring Great People*, through its many drafts, and finally during the process of editing and publishing this book, we have had the encouragement and assistance of many generous and talented people. While we can never thank them all, we would like to publicly acknowledge a few to whom we are particularly indebted.

This book could never have been written without the assistance of Select International's staff members Doug Wolf, Janice Marra, Deborah DeLuca, and Rosalyn Brancato. Their diligence, talent, and phenomenal ability to meet short deadlines kept us on schedule. Our thanks also go out to the many professionals who allowed us to learn from them, interview them, and write about them. Their words and stories give life to the ideas in this book.

We owe a special debt of gratitude to Jeanne Wilson, who connected us with John Woods of CWL Publishing Enterprises, our agent and editor. His vision helped us to put our passion, knowledge, and many years of experience into a book that will help managers make better hiring decisions. His enthusiastic support and guidance were invaluable. Also at CWL, Bob Magnan did a terrific job in editing the manuscript and checking the pages of the final product.

Most important, we want to thank our families, loved ones, and friends, whose quiet contributions will never be known, except by us.

About the Authors

Kevin C. Klinvex is a founding partner of Select International and Director of U.S. Operations. Over the past decade Kevin has designed cutting-edge staffing programs for leading companies including AK Steel, AT&T, Citibank, Coca-Cola, General Motors, International Harvester, Miller Brewing, Sears, Subaru-Isuzu, and Toyota. He has pioneered techniques for recruiting hard-to-find employees and is a thought leader in the use of software automation in the hiring process. Kevin is a frequent presenter and guest lecturer on the topic of staffing in a team environment.

Matthew S. O'Connell is a co-founder of Select International and Director of Research and Development. Over the past 12 years he has designed computerized assessment systems, 360 degree evaluation tools, behavioral interviews, and managerial assessment centers for over 100 companies in 7 countries. He is an adjunct professor of psychology at San Diego State University and is actively involved in applied research. He is author or co-author of over 20 articles or book chapters on selection and assessment, leadership, and teams. He received his master's and doctorate in Industrial and Organizational Psychology from the University of Akron.

Christopher P. Klinvex is a founding partner of Select International and is Director of International Operations and is responsible for Select's Monterrey, Mexico office. His experience with multinational companies includes the design and implementation of countrywide automated staffing systems, analysis of labor markets, strategic business planning sessions, design of teams, leadership training, management/labor mediation, and helping organizations understand the cultural nuances between traditional U.S. and Latin American work cultures.

Competency-Based Job Descriptions

Vexelle Manufacturing Inc. decided to build its second plant in a fairly small town in the Midwest. The new plant was going to have the best equipment, with all the latest technology. The first positions to be filled were for 15 maintenance workers. Sherri, the human resources manager for the new plant, was in charge of finding candidates to be interviewed by the maintenance and production managers. The response to an ad in the local paper was incredible: hundreds of candidates replied. After four days of interviewing, only three job offers had been made, and only one candidate accepted.

What happened?

Everyone had a different idea about what a "qualified" candidate looked like. The HR manager used an old job description to help her decide who to schedule for interviews. The maintenance manager felt that, with the new equipment, Programmable Logic Controls (PLC) experience was definitely a job requirement, and therefore eliminated all candidates without that particular skill. The production manager thought that training in PLC skills would be provided by the company, so he didn't even ask about PLC knowledge. Instead, he focused on the candidates' ability to work with others, because he was planning to implement a team-based work environment. Since everyone was evaluating the candidates against different criteria, there was no agreement about who to hire. The end result was that Vexelle had devoted extensive time and resources to a selection process that yielded only one hire.

In this chapter, you will learn the first step in developing a structured selection system that can help identify "qualified" candidates. Specifically, we'll provide answers to the following questions:

- How can a job description accurately define today's "work"?
- What does a competency-based job description look like?
- How do you identify "critical competencies"?
- How can a success profile help you select better workers?

How Can a Job Description Accurately Define Today's "Work"?

Everyone needs a job! Millions of job seekers scan the employment sections of the Sunday newspapers regularly, seeking that perfect job. Headhunters spend their careers trying to fill jobs. The 1990s is the decade of too many "jobs" and not enough candidates who can actually do the "work." Yet with all this talk about "jobs," we are seeing a surprising trend away from discussing jobs in the traditional sense.

Traditionally, companies defined a job by a specific set of tasks, duties, and responsibilities, listed in the form of a job description. The job description let employees know exactly what they were expected to do on the job. It also helped the company make hiring decisions. A candidate's background and experiences were compared with the job description. Often, with this approach, "experience performing the tasks in similar settings" was a major criterion that managers would use. Although this approach has worked for many companies over the years, today it is becoming obsolete.

The world of work has gone through some dramatic changes. Many of us have experienced the trauma of some sort of a "sizing" (whether it's downsizing, upsizing, or rightsizing). The objective is always the same—to find more productive ways to do the work! Increased productivity often requires a more flexible workforce—one that is multiskilled and able to perform more than one job. Yesterday's singularly focused job descriptions just can't capture the full array of skills, abilities, and motivations necessary for tomorrow's workforce.

Why Should I Develop Job Descriptions?

Don't misinterpret what we've said so far about job descriptions. We are not saying that you should do away with them. On the contrary, I strongly suggest that you do create job descriptions. However, the nature of today's job descriptions should reflect the nature of today's work. Let's take a look at some reasons why we still need job descriptions.

Ever try sending a friend to the grocery store without a list of exactly what you want? Breakfast cereals may be breakfast cereals, but there clearly are different types. Ever try to fill a position and have the hiring manager reject your top candidate? You and the hiring manager need to be reading from the same list of job requirements. A good job description can serve as the basis for developing structured selection tools that will help you identify the best candidates.

Candidates want to know what is expected of them and how they will be evaluated. A good job description is the basis of any performance evaluation system.

The value of any job can be traced back to the job description. You will need information when presenting the case for how much a job candidate should be paid. Without the job description, your guess will be as good as anyone's regarding how much to pay the new employee.

The job description also serves as a reality check! Too often we ask for individuals who do not exist in our job market or in the job's salary range. So we waste a lot of time searching for job candidates who, even if they did exist, would never take the position at the salary we are offering. Run your job description by other HR professionals or headhunters. This will ensure that if the job candidates do exist, you will not be wasting your time by offering them noncompetitive wages.

As you can see, the reasons why we need good job descriptions haven't really changed that much over the years. What has changed is what makes a job description "good" (i.e., accurate and useful).

What Should I Be Looking For?

A good job description accurately reflects the work that employees will be expected to perform. In the past, a good job description specifically outlined the duties, tasks, and responsibilities that the employee would perform in the position. This made sense. Job duties were fairly static, and jobs were distinct from one another.

Today, it's not unusual for companies to have 100 or more specific job titles, based on varying tasks and duties. The human resources department of such companies could spend months developing specific job descriptions for each of these titles. This doesn't make sense. In addition, the duties and tasks of today's jobs are more fluid and dynamic. Employees are expected to wear many hats—whatever it takes to help the company achieve its goals. This is another reason why job descriptions cannot be as narrowly defined as in the past. But how can we accurately define work without writing a description for every position that involves different duties and tasks?

First, we need to look at work in a broader sense than we have in the past. Traditionally, it was appropriate to ask, "What tasks, duties, and responsibilities are required to perform the job well?" Today, it's more appropriate to ask, "What *competencies* are required to succeed on the job?"

For instance, "leadership" is a competency that may require knowl-

> **Key Term**
>
> **Competencies** These are "clusters" of related knowledge, skills, abilities, motivations, and other requirements necessary for successful job performance.

Knowledge The information that an employee must possess to effectively perform the required work. This should not include specific knowledge that will be learned on the job. For example, a Spanish translator may need to have knowledge of technical vocabulary.

Skills and Abilities A level of expertise reflected in performance in relevant areas. Examples of *technical* skills and abilities are welding, tool and die work, drafting, technical writing, and accounting. Examples of *nontechnical* skills and abilities are planning and organizing, oral communication, interpersonal, decision making, and leadership.

Motivations Characteristics that motivate an employee to perform well on the job. (This topic is covered in detail in Chapter 8.) For instance, a successful salesperson may need to find satisfaction in interacting with many different types of people, working on commission, and conducting presentations.

Other Requirements If it doesn't fit one of the other three categories, you can stick it here. Legal documents such as certificates or licenses are included in this category.

edge of various management techniques, effective verbal communication skills, the ability to inspire and empower others, and the motivation to be a change agent.

By including competencies and a broader range of responsibilities in the job description, a number of HR functions can benefit. To begin with, a competency-based job description will provide greater flexibility in assigning work to your employees, allow you to group multiple jobs that require similar competencies under a single job description, and lengthen the life cycle of your job descriptions.

What Does a Competency-Based Job Description Look Like?

There are several key elements that make up a good job description. These include:

- **Job Title:** The title normally found on the new employee's business card or the term used to refer to his or her position. In a traditional or stable environment, the job title would be specific (e.g., Second Shift Supervisor, Cab Trim Department). In a flexible environment, the job title could be used for all supervisors, regardless of shift or department (e.g., Team Leader).

- **Relevance of the Position:** A statement about how the position supports the company business plan and its objectives. It would be much broader in a flexible environment than in a traditional environment.
- **Major Responsibilities:** A list of the primary work functions that the individual must do on a regular basis. In a traditional job description, this section would include a list of very specific tasks and duties to be performed regularly (e.g., review production goals with team members at the beginning of each shift). A more flexible job description would include broader responsibilities (e.g., facilitate team meetings).
- **Critical Criteria:** The standards that all job candidates must meet to be considered for the position. This is a key area for selection purposes. In traditional job descriptions, this section would include only specific requirements (e.g., work 2:30 to 11:30 p.m., level 3 operator status, able to lift 20 lb). A more flexible job description would include critical competencies required for the job (e.g., excellent teamwork skills, technical knowledge, ability to learn mul-

---

Smart Managing

Operating Procedures

The very detailed tasks and duties that make up the various parts of today's multi-faceted positions can be captured in a separate document called Operating Procedures. These documents will allow you to have a small number of shorter competency-based job descriptions while still capturing the critical tasks and duties of each job. Operating Procedures are useful for training and maintaining consistent work behavior. Unlike job descriptions, Operating Procedures are designed to be continuously updated to reflect changes in how specific parts of the job are performed.

tiple jobs, demonstrated ability to successfully coach and develop others, flexibility to work various shifts).

- **Preferred Criteria:** The qualities that you would like all candidates to possess, but that are not essential for successfully doing the job. These may look similar for a traditional or a flexible job description (e.g., five years' experience in the automotive industry, computer literate).
- **Reports to:** The position to which this hire would report (e.g., Group Leader).

Make Sure Your Job Descriptions Are Accurate

From a practical perspective, job descriptions are meaningless if they do not fit the job. This is where many companies get into trouble. If descriptions are not accurate, they can be misleading. Remember that the Critical Criteria section of the job description is the primary standard used in the hiring process.

The best hiring systems use the competencies identified in the Critical Criteria section of the job description as the basis for developing interview questions (see Chapters 6 and 7), identifying appropriate selection tests (see Chapter 9), and making the final hiring decision (see Chapter 11). The bottom line is,

> **⚠ CAUTION!**
>
> ### Make Them Job-Related
>
> The law requires that all criteria used for selection purposes be job-related. If someone in your company rejects a candidate based on an inaccurate job description, your company is a prime target for a lawsuit.

if your descriptions are inaccurate, your selection criteria will be inaccurate; if your selection criteria are inaccurate, your selection decisions will be inaccurate.

The rest of this chapter will show you the steps to take to build a solid foundation for developing a comprehensive and accurate selection system.

How Do I Identify "Critical Competencies"?

To get an accurate picture of the criteria that are critical to effective job performance, you must conduct a *Competency*

Competency Analysis The process by which you determine the competencies (knowledge, skills, abilities, motivations, and other requirements) necessary to perform a job successfully.

Success Profile A description of the competencies that are required for success in a particular job.

Analysis. The results of the competency analysis will serve as the basis for developing a success profile for the job.

A single success profile is often applicable to multiple positions within the same level in an organization. For instance, all first-level leadership positions in a manufacturing plant (i.e., team leaders) will likely require the same critical competencies for success. The tasks and duties may differ, but the same competencies are required.

Conducting a Competency Analysis

The key here is that you don't need to do a competency analysis for every job title in your company. In order to narrow your focus, you need to concentrate on job *levels* rather than job *titles.* Entry (e.g., hourly clerical and production positions), Intermediate (e.g., supervisors, team leaders), and Senior (e.g., mid- to upper-level managers) are examples of organizational levels. Within each level, specific jobs are then grouped into "job families." A job family is a group of positions, within the same organizational level, that have similar roles in achieving the organization's objectives. The focus of your competency analysis will be on a particular "job family."

Once you have identified your targeted job family, you can conduct the competency analysis. In order to conduct a thorough competency analysis, you will need to gather information from multiple sources—people who have a good understand-

Job Content Experts (JCEs) People who have expert knowledge of the tasks, duties, and requirements of the job. Experienced employees currently in the position and supervisors of the position usually make very good JCEs.

Analyzing Competencies

A manufacturing company has 2,500 employees. Three levels of positions have been identified within the organization: Hourly, Supervisory, and Senior. Within the Hourly level positions, there are three job families: Clerical, Production Associate, and Maintenance Technician positions. The company is interested in developing a selection system to evaluate candidates for its Production Associate positions. It will conduct a competency analysis to determine the knowledge, skills, abilities, and motivations required for success as a Production Associate. Later, the firm plans to conduct competency analyses for the Clerical and Maintenance Technician positions.

ing of the positions that you are analyzing. Such people are called *job content experts* or *JCEs*.

The first step in performing a competency analysis is to compile a detailed description of the tasks that make up the job. This is sometimes referred to as a "task analysis." Several data collection methods should be used, including:

Job Observation: Observe incumbents (i.e., people who are currently doing the job) performing their jobs. Watch what they are doing and ask them to describe what they are doing. Record their responses in detail.

Incumbent Interviews: Conduct interviews with people who are currently doing the job. Each incumbent should be asked the same questions, so you will need to develop the interview questions ahead of time. Your questions should focus on learning about their key responsibilities, the types of problems they need to solve, the interactions they have with others, the most difficult part of their job, and the skills and abilities they feel are necessary for success.

Critical Incidents Meetings: Facilitate meetings with job content experts (usually, the supervisors of the people in the target position). Ask them to provide specific examples of times when employees in that job demonstrated highly effective and highly ineffective behaviors. Here, you are focusing

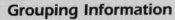

Grouping Information

To illustrate how knowledge, skills, abilities, and motivations are grouped, consider the following task analysis for the Production Associate position.

Production associates were observed working together in small teams and rotating jobs.

Incumbent interviews revealed that team members need to communicate to make sure that everything is done correctly.

The critical incidents meeting produced this example of a high performer: "Last week, Jodi took the time to give a new teammate some tips for doing his job more efficiently. During her break, she talked to the new employee to see how things were going and offered words of encouragement. She has done this on multiple occasions with new employees."

During the visioning session, employees were told about a continuous improvement initiative to begin within the next few months. Employees would volunteer to form multidisciplinary teams to address inefficiencies throughout the plant. Teams that met their goals would receive rewards.

The key knowledge, skills, abilities, and motivations gathered included "working together," "communicating," "offering encouragement," and "volunteering to form multidisciplinary teams." It was decided to group these competencies under the heading "Teamwork."

on traits that distinguish high performers from low performers. Record their examples in detail.

Competency Visioning Meetings: Facilitate meetings with people in the organization who are "visionaries"—people who really know the jobs, the organization, and, most important, the *future* of the jobs and the organization. Remember you are not only hiring for today. You want the people you hire today to still be around tomorrow. The purpose of this meeting is to gather information about the tasks that will be important for future success on the job, as well as to determine the knowledge, skills, abilities, motivations, and other requirements needed to accomplish those tasks.

Once you collect the data using the various methods described above, you need to analyze what you've got. That means grouping similar knowledge, skills, abilities, and motivations under headings, or *competencies.*

After analyzing all the data, you will have a list of competencies. This is where you need to be reasonable. Managers tend to come up with a lot of competencies. Once the list gets too long, there's bound to be overlap. For example, the skills and abilities needed to plan a project, schedule workers, and organize inventory are similar in that they can all be captured under a single heading like "Planning" or "Organizing." Your goal is to minimize overlap among competencies. When competencies are distinct from one another, it is easier to measure them with various selection tools. The easier they are to measure, the more accurate your results will be in terms of predicting job performance.

The competency analysis generates the success profile for the position. This success profile can serve as the foundation for improving (and integrating) a variety of HR functions, including selection, performance evaluations, training and development, and compensation.

> ## Position Competencies
> *TRICKS OF THE TRADE*
>
> As a general rule of thumb, the following guidelines can help you determine an appropriate number of position competencies.
>
> Entry-level hourly positions (clerical, manufacturing, service) usually require about 5 to 8 competencies.
>
> Intermediate-level positions (supervisor, team leader, professional) usually require about 8 to 11 competencies.
>
> Senior-level positions (mid- to upper-level managers, directors, advanced professionals) usually require about 10 to 14 competencies.

How Can a Success Profile Help Me Select Better Workers?

You'll remember the opening scenario, in which Vexelle was opening a plant and everyone involved in the selection process had a different idea of what the critical competencies were for the maintenance technician position. Now let's see how things could have turned out differently if Vexelle had done a thorough competency analysis and developed a success profile for the maintenance position.

Four months prior to opening the second manufacturing plant, the human resources department at Vexelle decided to take a good look at the jobs in the new plant. One major difference between the two plants was the technology. The new plant was going to have the most up-to-date equipment available. The new equipment would make the work less physically demanding than it was in the original facility. On the other hand, because employees in the new plant were going to work in teams, the production manager anticipated that other skills would be more important than in the past, such as communication and problem-solving skills.

The members of the human resources department decided to conduct a competency analysis for the maintenance positions at the new facility. They observed maintenance workers, interviewed them, facilitated critical incidents meetings, held visionary sessions, and analyzed data from a survey that asked job content experts to rate the importance of various competencies for effective job performance. The resulting success profile was composed of seven competencies, including technical skills, safety orientation, problem solving, and teamwork.

The success profile was incorporated into the Critical Criteria section of the job description and used as the basis for hiring maintenance workers. That is, each competency in the success profile was evaluated during the hiring process, using interviews and job-related tests.

Each candidate went through a technical test (designed to assess PLC programming knowledge) and a problem-solving test. Those who passed the tests were interviewed by Sherri, the HR manager. Sherri's interviews focused on several of the key competency areas. Those candidates who most closely matched the success profile were then interviewed by the production manager and the maintenance supervisor. Each asked every candidate a set of questions that focused on the critical competencies. Of the fifteen candidates who were granted final interviews, nine received offers and eight accepted!

Now I can't guarantee that you'll get similar results, even if you do a thorough competency analysis. Hiring ratios (and the success of those hired) depend on many factors, including your recruiting strategies (see Chapter 3), your selection tools (see Chapters 6, 7, 8, and 9), and your job offer (see Chapter 12). However, structuring a selection system based on a thorough competency analysis will always help you achieve better results. "Better results" means hiring employees who are more likely to succeed on the job—and protecting your company against lawsuits!

What does it take to be a successful salesperson with your company? A great supervisor? A skilled maintenance technician? An outstanding customer service representative? Do you have a clear picture of the success profiles of the positions in your organization?

Determine Your Priorities

The results of a competency analysis can be applied to a single function (i.e., selection system, performance evaluation, pay scales, training, etc.), or they can be used to integrate HR systems. Basically, ask yourself, "What do I plan to do with the success profiles?"

The next step is to group jobs that have similar functions. Groups of jobs with similar functions are sometimes referred to as *job families*.

Determine which job families are in need of selection system improvements. In which jobs are there problems with turnover, absenteeism, production, quality, or customer service? If you keep your eyes and ears open, you're bound to know exactly where the problems are occurring.

Conduct a competency analysis for your target position.

Make sure your selection tools are capable of evaluating all of the critical competencies in the success profile.

Update your job descriptions by including competencies from the analysis in the Critical Criteria section.

Think of the success profile as the gauge by which all candidates will be measured. Figure out the acceptable levels for each job competency, according to the requirements of the job and the selection tools used. When a thorough competency analysis is conducted and valid selection tools are used (see Chapters 6, 7, 8, and 9), competencies can be powerful predictors of performance on the job.

Manager's Checklist for Chapter 1

❑ Job descriptions are still important in the hiring process, but the question "What duties, tasks, and responsibilities are involved in this job?" has become "What *competencies* are required to succeed on the job?"

❑ You need a competency-based job description that will provide greater flexibility in assigning work, allow you to group jobs that require similar competencies under a single job description, and lengthen the life cycle of your job descriptions.

❑ A competency-based job description includes the job title, the relevance of the position, the major responsibilities (general), critical criteria, and preferred criteria.

❑ Identify critical competencies by conducting a competency analysis, a process by which you determine the knowledge, skills, abilities, motivations, and other requirements necessary to perform a job successfully.

Legal Issues

Jim, the HR manager, and Jerry, the plant manager at Rapco Industries, had a very straightforward approach to hiring employees. They would interview each candidate and, if they both agreed that the person was good, they would hire him or her. Jim was pretty structured in the questions he would ask, but Jerry had a more intuitive approach to interviewing. With 20 years' experience in manufacturing, Jerry knew what it took to perform the job.

Last month, Jim received a letter notifying him that Lisa Smith, a candidate for one of their manufacturing positions, had filed a complaint with the EEOC and was pursuing legal action against Rapco. Jim and Jerry had not offered Lisa a position, although her employment record was outstanding. As the case progressed, it was revealed that Jerry had asked Lisa if her husband would approve of her working in a plant and commented that his experience was that women didn't last long in the manufacturing positions at Rapco.

Lisa ended up winning the case and a position at Rapco. Rapco's legal bill for the case (including attorney fees for both parties) was over $80,000. Quite a costly hire, when all was said and done.

What happened?

Lisa was treated differently from other applicants for the position. Given Jerry's question and comment during the interview, Lisa believed that she was denied employment based on her gender. The EEOC also believed that there was evidence to suggest that Rapco's hiring practices might be discriminatory against women. And, ultimately, the court agreed.

While the opening scenario is fictitious, cases like these are argued, and won, every day.

You can avoid the legal liability of employment discrimination if you know and follow the laws that regulate hiring practices. Being aware and informed can save your business time and money. In this chapter, you will become acquainted with some of the basic legal issues associated with hiring:

- Discrimination in Hiring
- The EEOC
- Title VII of the Civil Rights Act (1964)
- Age Discrimination in Employment Act (1967)
- Immigration Reform and Control Act (1990)
- Americans with Disabilities Act (1990)
- Civil Rights Act (1991)

Discrimination in Hiring

Many laws have been enacted to protect individuals from discrimination and to provide equal employment opportunities (EEO).

With respect to the hiring process, discrimination refers to distinctions made on the basis of what we will refer to as "protected characteristics" that have no relationship to job performance.

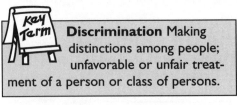

Discrimination Making distinctions among people; unfavorable or unfair treatment of a person or class of persons.

Protected *characteristics* (e.g., color of skin) should be distinguished from protected *groups* (e.g., African Americans). For example, the protection against racial discrimination is not limited to members of any particular race. Whites also are protected under Title VII of the Civil Rights Act of 1964, as amended. "Reverse discrimination" cases (cf., *Regents of University of California vs. Bakke 438 U.S.265, 1978*) highlight the need to avoid making decisions based on protected characteristics, no matter which group the discrimination favors.

> **Protected characteristics** Characteristics that are covered under antidiscrimination employment laws. There are six broad categories of protected characteristics, including race and color, gender, religion, national origin, age (over 40), and disabilities.

It's important to note that federal EEO laws do not require an employer to give *preferential treatment* to any person or group of persons because of race, color, religion, sex, national origin, age, or disability. However, they do demand that all persons receive the *same opportunities* for employment.

There are two types of discrimination. The most obvious form of discrimination is called *disparate treatment*, or unequal treatment.

In a disparate treatment case, the plaintiff must prove that he or she (1) is protected by a relevant EEO statute, (2) was qualified for the job, and (3) was not hired, while the job remained open to other similarly qualified candidates. The scenario opening this chapter is an example of disparate treatment. As illustrated in that example, all you have to do is ask a candidate a question that you don't ask of all the other candidates,

> **Disparate Treatment** Treating people differently based on "protected characteristics." This is relatively obvious discrimination. While this type of discrimination is usually viewed as deliberate, it does not necessarily require malicious intent.

and you can be accused of disparate treatment. As you will see throughout this book, developing a structured selection system that is applied consistently for every candidate is vital to protecting your company against such litigation.

The second type of discrimination is *adverse impact*. This type of discrimination is sometimes referred to as *disparate impact*.

The following example summarizes an actual lawsuit that was successfully litigated using adverse impact as an argument.

> **Key Term**
>
> **Adverse Impact** A hiring practice that disproportionately discriminates against a group of persons based on "protected characteristics." The hiring practice usually appears to be neutral (i.e., non-discriminatory) and the resulting discrimination can be intentional or unintentional.

A company seeking candidates for entry-level management positions required a pre-employment skills test to measure math and grammar skills, reading comprehension, and the ability to follow orders. A Hispanic applicant was not hired because he failed the test. He was told he could retake the test in six months, but he felt the test was discriminatory and filed a lawsuit against the company.

The test was judged discriminatory to the applicant by an appeals court (*Melendez v. Illinois Bell Tel. Co.,* 7th *Cir., 79 F.3d 661, 1996*). The test was shown to have adverse impact against Hispanics and African Americans, as shown by the following pass rates: 77% of white applicants, 47% of Hispanics, and 22% of African Americans. Even more damaging to the defense, an outside expert found that there was no significant correlation between employees' test scores and their subsequent job performance. The expert concluded that the test predicted job performance only 3% better than chance alone and was not job-related.

As this example illustrates, adverse impact can occur even with seemingly neutral hiring practices. To show that a test has adverse impact, a statistic referred to as the "Four-Fifths Rule" is a useful index. You first calculate the pass rate for the majority group of applicants. Then, you multiply the majority group's pass rate by 4/5 or 80%. If the pass rate for a protected group of applicants is lower than this number, the test can

> ### How Four-Fifths Works
> To show how the "Four-Fifths Rule" works, consider
> this example. Let's say that a company tested several
> hundred applicants for customer service positions and that the
> majority of applicants were white. You find that 60% of whites
> pass the test. If we multiply 60% by 4/5, we get 48%. This 48%
> is used as the minimum pass rate for all other racial groups to
> avoid claims of adverse impact. For instance, if the pass rate for
> African Americans were 50%, there would be *no* adverse
> impact against African Americans. If the pass rate for Hispanics
> were 42%, there *would be* adverse impact against Hispanics.

be said to have adverse impact against that group.

Demonstrating that a test has adverse impact against a
protected group does not necessarily mean that the company
is guilty of discrimination. This is where the company needs to
have done its research. To defend against adverse impact
claims, there must first be
evidence that the test is
related to job perfor-
mance. An expert in the
field of industrial psychology can conduct studies
that show whether or not
this relationship exists.
Next, there must be no
alternative test that is *as*

> ### Be Proactive
> Don't wait until you are faced
> with a lawsuit to build a
> defense against adverse impact.
> Involve an industrial psychologist early
> on to ensure that your selection
> tools are job-related and have no
> adverse impact.

related to job performance as the one used and that has less
adverse impact. Essentially, the courts have said that if there
is an equally valid test that has less adverse impact, the company should have known about it and used it instead.

The EEOC

The Equal Employment Opportunity Commission (EEOC),
established in 1965, interprets and enforces federal statutes
regarding employment discrimination. The mission of the
EEOC is "to promote equal opportunity in employment by

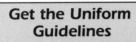

Get the Uniform Guidelines

Smart Managing For a copy of the Uniform Guidelines in Employee Selection Procedures, contact the EEOC: Office of Equal Employment Opportunity, 1801 L St., NW, Washington, DC 20507. You can call the EEOC toll-free at 1-800-669-EEOC (voice) or 1-800-800-3302 (TDD). For calls from the Washington, DC, metropolitan area, dial (202) 663-4900 (voice) or (202) 663-4494 (TDD).

enforcing the federal civil rights employment laws through administrative and judicial actions, and education and technical assistance." The EEOC's key document is the Uniform Guidelines in Employee Selection Procedures.

Usually, applicants who feel they have been discriminated against will contact the EEOC or the state Fair Employment Practices Commission. The agency contacted will review the complaint to determine if there is a *prima facie* case. Basically, this means that the agency determines whether or not there is enough evidence to proceed with a case. If there's prima facie evidence, the agency will intervene for the plaintiff. Otherwise, the person may still pursue the case, but without the support of the agency.

In this chapter, we will review five federal EEO statutes that have had the greatest impact on hiring practices.

Make Sure You Comply

It is not the intent of this chapter to provide legal advice. There are numerous federal, state, and local laws and regulations, as well as court rulings that apply to hiring practices that are not covered in this book. It is always wise to review your current policies with an employment law specialist who has expertise in EEOC regulations, as well as state and any local employment laws that could affect your business.

Title VII of the Civil Rights Act (1964)

Title VII of the Civil Rights Act protects individuals against employment discrimination on the basis of race and color, national origin, gender, or religion. This is the big one. It was the first federal statute to protect against discrimination in employment, and it continues to have significant impact on hiring practices today. It prohibits both intentional discrimination and the use of seemingly neutral hiring practices that disproportionately exclude minorities and that are not job-related. Title VII covers federal, state, and local governments, educational institutions, and private employers that have 15 or more employees. Private and public employment agencies, labor organizations, and joint labor-management committees for apprenticeship and training must also abide by the law. If your business falls under the jurisdiction of Title VII, you are required to keep employment records for a period of six months beginning on the day you created a record of any candidate for employment. This includes application forms and all data relating to the hiring process.

There are numerous topics that relate to characteristics protected under Title VII and other antidiscrimination laws. Some of these topics may appear to be "neutral" in that they are topics that may come up during the course of normal conversation. However, the rules that apply to "normal conversation" are not the same rules that apply to an employment interview or any other hiring practice. For this reason, it is very important that you become familiar with all of the topics that might be perceived by someone to be "potentially discriminatory." To this end, let's take a closer look at each of the characteristics protected under Title VII and related topics that you should avoid when interacting with applicants.

Race, Color, and National Origin

Under Title VII, it is unlawful to discriminate against a job applicant based on his or her race, color, or national origin. The following topics relate to race, color, or national origin and should *not* be asked about or used as criteria *in the hiring process*. Keep in mind that this list is not all-inclusive.

- Race
- Color
- Ethnicity

- Ethnic association or surname
- Nation of origin
- Birthplace of candidate or candidate's relatives
- Candidate's native tongue
- Whether candidate is a citizen of another country
- Linguistic characteristics or accents
- Physical characteristics (e.g., hair texture or facial features)
- Any condition that occurs more often in one particular racial/ethnic group (e.g., sickle cell anemia)

Gender

Under Title VII, you are required to treat men and women equally in the selection process unless there is a job-related reason for giving an advantage to either. Restricting the employment of married women and unmarried men, for example, is sexual discrimination, since gender is the key factor. An exception can be made if the job factor is a Bona Fide Occupational Qualification (BFOQ).

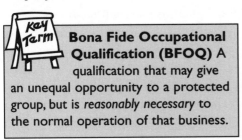

Bona Fide Occupational Qualification (BFOQ) A qualification that may give an unequal opportunity to a protected group, but is *reasonably necessary* to the normal operation of that business.

An example of a BFOQ is requiring male attendants in a men's lavatory and female attendants in a women's lavatory. However, BFOQs are generally difficult to prove for most positions.

The following topics relate to gender and should *not* be asked about or used as criteria *in the hiring process.* Keep in mind that this list is not all-inclusive.

- Gender
- Marital status
- Maiden name
- Family plans
- Number of children
- Occupation of spouse or other relatives

- Health care coverage through spouse
- Child care arrangements
- Whom to contact in case of an emergency
- Sexual preference

An amendment to Title VII, The Pregnancy Discrimination Act, prohibits discrimination on the basis of pregnancy, childbirth, or related medical conditions. You may not refuse to hire a woman because of any pregnancy-related condition, as long as she is able to perform the essential job functions.

Religion

Under Title VII, an employer cannot discriminate against an applicant based on religious practices or beliefs. In addition, an employer cannot schedule examinations or other selection activities that may conflict with a prospective employee's religious needs.

The following topics relate to religion and should *not* be asked about or used as criteria *in the hiring process*. Keep in mind that this list is not all-inclusive.

- Religious affiliation
- Religious holidays observed
- Religious practices
- Church/synagogue/mosque/temple attendance
- Religious activities

Age Discrimination in Employment Act of 1967 (ADEA)

The Age Discrimination in Employment Act protects individuals who are 40 years of age or older from any condition of employment based on age. The ADEA applies to employers with 20 or more employees, including federal, state, and local governments, employment agencies, and labor organizations.

While the ADEA does not specifically prohibit employers from asking an applicant's age or date of birth, this type of inquiry may indicate a possible intent to discriminate and would be closely scrutinized for a lawful purpose.

Is age discrimination always illegal? No. You may ask if a candidate is of legal age (such as 18 or 21) to do a job. But the ADEA makes it unlawful to include age preferences, limitations, or specifications in your job notices or advertisements.

The following topics relate to age and should *not* be asked about or used as criteria *in the hiring process*. Keep in mind that this list is not all-inclusive.

- Candidate's age
- Date of birth
- Date of high school graduation
- Number of grandchildren
- Ages of children/grandchildren
- Social Security/Senior Citizen benefits
- Retirement plans

Immigration Reform and Control Act of 1990 (IRCA)

The Immigration Reform and Control Act applies to all employers in the United States and prohibits discrimination based on national origin or citizenship.

Under this act, the employer must obtain verification of an applicant's right to work in the United States. Note that U.S. citizenship is *not* required in most cases. If you impose citizenship requirements or give preference to U.S. citizens in hiring or employment opportunities, you may be in violation of IRCA, unless there is a legal requirement for a particular job.

> ### Get Information about IRCA
> Smart Managing You can find out more about employment rights and responsibilities under the Immigration Reform and Control Act by calling the Office of Special Counsel for Immigration Related Unfair Employment Practices. The toll-free number is 1-800-255-7688 (voice) or 1-800-237-2525 (TDD).

Usually, employers will collect documents of verification to work in the United States only from applicants to whom they have made an offer. But regardless of when you collect this information, the key is to be consistent. If you single out individuals of a particular national origin, or individuals who *appear* to be foreign, to provide employment verification, you may be in violation of both IRCA and Title VII. Therefore, if you decide to collect verification from a particular candidate who "looks foreign" before you conduct the final interview, you better collect it from *every* candidate *before* the final interview.

Americans with Disabilities Act of 1990 (ADA)

The Americans with Disabilities Act prohibits discrimination against a qualified individual with a disability. To comply with the ADA, you are required to keep all materials relating to the hiring process for one year from the date of action.

The ADA covers physical or mental impairments that substantially limit major life activities. *Physical impairments* include physiological disorders or conditions, cosmetic disfigurement, or an anatomical loss. *Mental impairments* include mental or psychological disorders such as mental retardation, emotional or mental illness, and specific learning disabilities. *Major life activities* are

> **Disability** A physical or mental impairment that substantially limits one or more major life activities. This term also applies to any person who has a record of such an impairment or is believed to have such an impairment.

such functions as breathing, seeing, hearing, speaking, caring for oneself, performing manual tasks, walking, learning, and working.

A *qualified* individual with a disability is one who, with or without *reasonable accommodation,* has the skills, experience, education, and other requirements of the job and can perform the *essential functions* of the job without endangering his or her health and safety or that of others.

There are numerous "reasonable accommodations" that employers can make to assist qualified individuals with disabilities in the performance of essential job functions. The following list provides some examples. Keep in mind that what

Reasonable accommodation A modification in a job's task or structure or in the workplace that will allow the qualified individual with a disability to perform the essential job functions and that does not place undue hardship on the employer.

Essential functions Activities that are critical to performing a particular job.

Undue hardship An action requiring significant difficulty or expense when considered in light of such factors as the employer's size, financial resources, and the nature and structure of the operation.

may be "reasonable" for one employer may not be for another. These may include:

- Making facilities accessible to and usable by individuals with disabilities (e.g., installing ramps and automatic doors)
- Job restructuring (e.g., remove a nonessential function)
- Offering part-time or modified work schedules (e.g., allowing Tuesday mornings off for therapy)
- Acquiring or modifying equipment or devices (e.g., using voice-activated computer software)
- Adjusting or modifying selection procedures (e.g., providing a reader or an interpreter)

Concerns about hiring a person with a disability often center around the person's ability to perform job duties and meet attendance requirements. However, when you think about it, employers have these concerns about *all* candidates.

A standard set of questions can be developed and used in the hiring process to identify whether or not each applicant (with or without a disability) is able to perform the essential job functions (with or without accommodation). The standard set of questions can be in the form of a list of essential job functions. For example, if the job requires lifting, an item on the checklist might read: "In this job, you will need to lift 50 lbs. Can you meet this requirement, with or without accommodation?" The interviewer simply reads each job function and asks the applicant if he or she can perform the function with or without accommodation. If the candidate indicates the need for an accommodation, the interviewer writes down a detailed description of it.

The ADA outlines several situations that employers may encounter when interacting with an applicant and what the employer may and may not ask. They are:

> ### Essential Functions Checklist
>
> If you have an essential functions checklist, use it with every candidate, not just those you believe might have a disability. Using a standard format will ensure that every candidate is asked the same questions in the same way. Similarly, if a job has physical requirements, don't require only certain candidates to take a medical exam. For every phase in your hiring process, your safest bet is to use a standard process and apply it consistently.

- If a candidate has a *known* disability (e.g., has one arm) that *would appear to interfere with or prevent performance of a job-related function* (e.g., placing bulky item on shelves up to 6 feet high), you *may* ask the candidate to describe how he or she would perform this function (even if other applicants do not have to do so). The focus should be on obtaining a complete description of the accommodation that would be needed in order for the candidate to perform the function.
- If a candidate has a *known* disability (e.g., uses a wheelchair) that *does not appear to interfere with a job function* (e.g., sort parts while seated), you *cannot* ask for a description of how he or she would perform the function.
- If you suspect a candidate has a *disability*, you cannot ask for a description of how he or she would perform the function.
- If a candidate *voluntarily indicates* that he or she would need accommodation to perform a task, you would be required to get a detailed description of the requested accommodation.

- If a candidate indicates that he or she *cannot perform an essential job function,* even with accommodation, the candidate would *not* be qualified for the job.

As you can see from the ADA guidelines summarized above, employers are *sometimes* allowed to ask how an individual will perform essential job functions. However, under the ADA, the employer is *never* allowed to ask an applicant about the disability itself. The ADA strictly prohibits inquiries about an applicant's disability during the preemployment process (applications, medical information forms, interviews, etc.). Such inquiries are prohibited to ensure that you don't screen out qualified individuals before you determine if they can perform the job.

The following topics relate to disabilities and should *not* be asked about or used as criteria *in the hiring process.* Keep in mind that this list is not all-inclusive.

Don't Violate the Law

Take the following steps to ensure that your selection system does not violate employment laws.

Consult an employment law expert to review your selection process, including the tools you use to screen and evaluate candidates and make hiring decisions.

Consult an industrial psychologist to review your selection tools to make sure all criteria are job-related and to eliminate any potential adverse impact.

Make sure that a job analysis (see Chapter 1) has been done and that your selection process relates to the results of that analysis.

Make sure that everyone involved in the hiring process is trained to do what they are assigned to do. Even the most legally defensible selection system can turn out to be legally "indefensible" if it is not administered properly and consistently.

Review your selection process regularly. Job requirements and employment legislation change over time. Your selection process may need to be modified to reflect these changes.

- Existence of a disability
- Nature or severity of any disability
- Cause of any disability
- Prognosis of any condition or disability
- Whether the applicant would need special leave because of any disability
- Whether the applicant has ever filed a worker's compensation claim
- Past, present, or future treatment by a medical doctor, psychiatrist, psychologist, or other medical professional
- Use of prescription drugs
- Treatment for alcohol or drug abuse
- Treatment for any specified conditions or diseases
- Major illnesses or surgeries
- Current state of mental or physical health
- Exercise or nutrition habits
- Physical characteristics (e.g., height, weight)

Civil Rights Act of 1991

The Civil Rights Act of 1991 allows an applicant to seek compensatory damages (for monetary and nonmonetary loss) and punitive damages (to punish the employer) for acts of discrimination based on gender, religion, and disability. It also provides for a jury trial for the plaintiff. This act does not extend protection to any characteristics not already covered under Title VII, but it does create steeper consequences for employers who violate it.

Bottom Line

Keep in mind that employment laws do more than just protect the applicants. They also help employers select applicants based on whether or not they can perform the job. That should be your ultimate goal. Your selection system should help you distinguish applicants who can do the job from those who cannot. This book is aimed at helping you develop a hiring process that will do just that.

Manager's Checklist for Chapter 2

❑ Title VII of Civil Rights Act (1964) prohibits discrimination in all conditions of employment based on *race, color, national origin, religion,* and *gender.*

❑ The Age Discrimination in Employment Act (1967) prohibits discrimination in employment for individuals age 40 and over.

❑ The Immigration Reform and Control Act (1990) prohibits discrimination based on national origin but also requires employers to obtain verification of an applicant's right to work in the United States.

❑ The Americans with Disabilities Act (1990) prohibits discrimination against a qualified individual with a disability. A *qualified* individual is one who can perform the essential functions of the job with or without reasonable accommodations.

❑ The Civil Rights Act (1991) allows an applicant to seek compensatory and punitive damages for willful discrimination.

Attracting the Right Employees

E ric sat staring at offer letters from Gore, Mirmax, and Connex. All three companies offered good pay, great benefits, opportunities for growth, and a pleasant work environment. All three had virtually the same package. But only Gore had communicated its "package" to Eric in a way that made him think of Gore as a great place to work. Which company do you think Eric went to work for? Where did Mirmax and Connex go wrong? What did Gore do right?

Have you ever lost an applicant (after spending thousands of dollars on recruiting) because he or she didn't perceive your company as a great place to work?

In this chapter, you'll learn about the following topics:
- What makes a company a great place to work?
- Which benefits do today's workers find most desirable?
- Assessing your company's package
- Choosing the right vehicle for your message
- Evaluating your recruiting efforts

Advertising

To understand why Eric chose Gore, let's walk through the recruiting process of the three companies.

Both Mirmax and Connex kicked off their recruiting campaign for a process engineer with traditional ads in the classified section of their local newspaper. Figure 3-1 shows the ad Connex placed in the classified section of the local newspaper. Mirmax ran a similar ad that also focused on the job duties and the education and experience required.

Process Engineer

Connex, a growing international company that engineers a variety of products using the latest technology, has an immediate opening for a process engineer. This position requires a B.S. in engineering and a minimum of 5 years' experience as a process engineer, preferably in the medical technology field. Successful process engineers will be team-oriented and have excellent analytical skills and creative problem-solving ability. Interested candidates should mail their résumés to: Connex, 2710 Appletree Rd., Hampton, MA 05555

Figure 3-1. The Connex ad

Compare this with the display ad that Gore ran in the business section of the newspaper (Figure 3-2). Teaser ads in the business and sports sections of the paper as well as radio spots directed readers to the classified section. The use of graphics enables the reader to feel the energy, and the text conveys the promise of this company. The enthusiasm practically leaps off the page!

The Gore ad says very little about job duties. In fact, it doesn't name a particular position because it's designed to recruit for several technical positions. Instead, the emphasis is on how technical positions can make a difference and how they tie in with Gore's vision to discover and develop breakthrough technology and get it to the market quickly.

Gore also ran radio spots during drive time to advertise the technical positions. These ads invited potential applicants to stop by on their way to work to have a cup of coffee and a bagel and learn more about Gore and the technical positions

Figure 3-2. The Gore ad

advertised. No appointment was necessary. Representatives spent 15 to 30 minutes with each person who stopped by.

A human resources associate and selected technical representatives were on hand to talk to Eric. This was important because the technical staff was able to communicate excitement about their work—in a language that Eric could relate to. All of Gore's staff was dressed informally, reflecting the dress code at Gore. That, combined with the relaxed setting of this drive-through get-acquainted session, helped Eric experience the friendly, informal, and supportive culture of Gore.

Gore offered Eric yet another opportunity to get to know them. The company ran newspaper display ads (again in the business section) and radio spots inviting potential applicants to join Gore at a Technical Career Information Session. This informational get-together gave applicants a couple of hours to spend with their prospective employer. (Note: résumés were optional.)

The Technical Career Information Session proved to be an interesting evening. A Gore human resources representative greeted Eric at the door. He signed in, giving his name, address, and phone number. (This was necessary since résumés were optional.) He was then given a choice of visiting one of seven subject matter tables or a career information session that began every half-hour.

Eric first visited the subject matter tables. There were seven different tables, each representing one of Gore's core technologies. Gore technical staff was on hand in each area to answer questions and conduct demonstrations. Gore products (and the products of the companies Gore supplies) were on display.

Next, Eric visited the career information session. It began with a slide show accompanied by soft music and featured a typical manufacturing setting. After a couple of minutes, the music stopped—just long enough to make everyone uncomfortable. Then the music started again—only this time it was louder (a full surround-sound system was used) and upbeat. The slides now revealed what manufacturing was like at Gore. Here again, Gore was letting Eric experience its culture and its technology.

The final part of the evening was spent with a human resources associate to schedule an interview. Gore expected approximately 150 people at the Technical Career Information Session. Over 300 attended. The buzz of all those people interested in working for Gore and the enthusiasm of the Gore staff made a lasting impression on Eric. He had a fun evening talking to people who did what he did—people he could relate to.

Eric scheduled an interview with Gore (as did 77 other visitors). Several days later, he received a letter from Gore, thanking him for attending the session. Meanwhile, he got calls from Mirmax and Connex in response to the résumés he'd mailed them. After a brief phone screen, both companies scheduled him for an interview. All three interviews took place the same week. Here's how they went.

Interviewing

At Mirmax, Eric was interviewed by Jim, the human resources manager. Jim was dressed in a suit and tie—not the way he normally dresses because Mirmax has a business-casual dress code. The interview, like the newspaper ad, focused on duties and expectations. Using a behavioral interviewing process, Jim collected valuable data about Eric's experience but never gave Eric an opportunity to "experience" what it would be like to work at Mirmax. Not once did Jim tell Eric how his "duties" would fit into the big picture at Mirmax. One of Mirmax's products had just been approved for use on the next space shuttle, but Jim made no mention of it. At the end of the interview, Jim gave Eric a brochure about Mirmax's products and a list of benefits and said he would call if a second interview were necessary.

Two days later, Eric interviewed with Connex. He met with Connex's human resources manager, Julie. Julie spent about 45 minutes with Eric. Many of the questions she asked seemed to Eric to be unrelated to the job he was interviewing for. After the interview with Julie, he had an interview with Richard, manager of process engineering.

Richard's monotone voice and poker-face style gave Eric the feeling that Richard was just going through the motions. Nothing could have been further from the truth. Richard's technical expertise on two projects this past year had enabled Connex to be first in the marketplace with a new stainless steel heart splint. Since Richard never revealed anything about his work, Eric felt that Richard was bored with either his job or Eric. Richard spent nearly an hour focusing on Eric's technical experience and qualifications but never demonstrated how either would fit into what Connex was trying to accomplish. Eric noticed that Richard asked many of the same questions Julie asked.

Both Julie and Richard failed to give Eric complete information on Connex's benefits package. It was the best of the three companies he was considering, but he left without knowing that.

The very next day Eric went to Gore. When Eric had scheduled the interview, he was given an agenda that told him the date and time of the interview, how much time to allow, and who would interview him. He was also given the names and functional responsibilities of the team of interviewers (all trained in behavioral interviewing)—Joe, the technical recruiter, and a core process engineering team consisting of a team leader and two highly respected associates. Just knowing this information made Eric feel more relaxed going into the interview.

Joe and the interview team had a game plan. They prepared interview guides based on the job analysis that had been done. Interview questions were divided so that each was collecting different information from Eric. In addition to the interview questions, Joe and each team member played an important role in making sure Eric left with the impression that Gore was a great place to work.

Joe's responsibility was to make sure that Eric would fit into Gore's unique culture. He wanted to encourage and answer (on the spot) any questions about Gore's general benefits package, job responsibilities, and culture. He also wanted to make sure Eric knew how much Gore wanted him to put his talents to work for them.

The process engineering team's role was to ensure that Eric could touch and feel his potential work environment. They wanted to make the job come alive for Eric so he could actually see himself in the Gore "big picture." They also wanted to clearly communicate to Eric the learning opportunities that exist, both formally and informally, within the company, and to inform him about the company's continuous learning philosophy.

Eric met first with Joe, who spent about an hour interviewing Eric about cultural fit (whether Eric would feel comfortable and could work well in Gore's corporate culture) and reviewing the benefits package. Eric spent the second hour interviewing with the process engineering team leader, who collected specific information on the types of projects Eric had experience with and told him about some of the new products Gore had recently developed. It was obvious to Eric (within minutes) that the team leader was excited about the difference that Gore's products would make in the world.

Next Eric was teamed up with two associates from process engineering—people he would actually be working with on a daily basis. Each explained to Eric the types of projects they were involved with and the responsibilities they have. They assured Eric there is no "pigeonholing" at Gore and as long as they take care of their core responsibilities, associates are encouraged to explore other areas. One of the engineering associates (with two years' experience) told Eric that he was working on projects for which other organizations would have required five or six years' experience. Gore's support of their innovative spirit and quest for excellence in their work was evident throughout the interview.

After Eric finished with the team of interviewers, there was no doubt in his mind that Gore would be a great place to work!

What Makes a Company a Great Place to Work?

It's a combination of monetary and nonmonetary rewards, of tangible and intangible benefits. It's the right mix, the right package. That's what makes a desirable applicant want to come to work for you.

Robert Levering, co-author of *The 100 Best Companies to Work for in America*, defines "a great place to work" as one where you "trust the people you work for, have

Judging Workplace Relationships

Here are sample statements from Levering's Trust Index, a tool used to measure people's perceptions of their workplace relationships—with management, with their jobs, and with other employees. Responses to statements like these measure credibility, respect, fairness, pride, and camaraderie.

• Management delivers on its promises.
• People are encouraged to balance their work life and their personal life.
• Promotions go to those who best deserve them.
• I'm proud to tell others I work here.
• I can be myself around here.

pride in what you do, and enjoy the people you work with." Levering's definition is based on extensive employee interviews he conducted for the 1984 and 1993 editions of his best-selling book.

Is your company a great place to work? If the answer is yes, by all means communicate it or, better yet, let applicants experience it—like Gore did. If you're not sure of how your company is perceived in the community, you may find the answer in a culture climate survey that your company should conduct annually. Just use a simple questionnaire asking what employees find most and least desirable about their job and workplace. You can even collect information from applicants. Provide a space on your application asking what attracted them to your company. Honest answers will help you get a good understanding of what you have to offer to a desirable applicant.

If you would like some help developing a questionnaire to use with your employees, there are numerous consulting firms that can provide you with "off-the-shelf" or customized surveys to meet your particular needs.

Which Benefits Do Employees Find Most Desirable?

While Levering's research concludes that the quality of workplace relationships is the top factor in determining a great place to work, benefits aren't far behind. According to Beth Boden, communications practice leader for Hewitt Associates, a leading management consulting firm, today's workers consider a company to have a good benefits package if it helps them with their needs, fears, and goals.

Needs, fears, and goals will vary with the age and demographics of your workforce. It's important to consider these three variables in determining what type of benefits your organization should offer. But pretty much across the board, employees today are looking for a *partnership* with an organization. And employers are responding in a variety of ways.

Many companies use pay-for-performance plans, such as individual bonuses or gain sharing, to help employees connect

Employees' Top Ten

Hewitt offers the following top ten employee priorities based on needs, fears, and goals. The list comes from focus studies done with employees across the country.

  1. Feeling secure in my job
  2. Having financial security
  3. Preparing for retirement
  4. Saving for child's tuition
  5. Saving for a home
  6. Retiring early
  7. Making more money
  8. Furthering my education outside of work
  9. Staying healthy
 10. Having more time for family

personal success with company success. Pension plans are also being structured in ways that tie them directly to the profits of the company. Even pension plan reports are being tied to performance. Companies distribute quarterly reports showing the cash balance of a pension plan, highlighting information on how profits are helping to boost (or drain) the cash balance.

Flexible benefits plans are also quite appealing to the majority of employees today. This is evident in the growing use of "cafeteria plans" that allow employees to choose from a range of options in everything from medical to retirement to time off. Medical plans may allow an employee to choose a dental or vision option. Some plans allow participants to set aside tax-free dollars to spend on medical expenses.

Retirement plans like a 401(k) plan enable employees to control where their money is invested. Paid-time-off pools allow employees to use all of their sick time, vacation time, and personal time as they need or want. The role of today's employer is to give employees access to benefits and then let employees decide what they want and how they'll use them.

In general, employees will consider a company to have a good benefits package if it includes the following:

On-Demand Information

Employees want information about their benefits on an on-time, on-demand basis. They want to be able to *retrieve* rather than *receive* information. Employers are taking advantage of technology to make this information readily available. Software, intranets, and advanced telecommunications systems make it easy and convenient for employees to retrieve everything from claim forms to a 401(k) balance. (No more thick employee benefits binders, please!) Some HR departments have a home page on the company intranet system so employees can retrieve and print information as needed.

- 401(k) or other matched employee retirement plan
- Medical plan
- Pension plan (funded by employer)
- Pay-for-performance compensation
- Flexible working hours
- Child care on- or off-site
- Tuition reimbursement

Which of these benefits does your company offer? Make a list. How does your benefits package compare with packages at companies you're competing with for applicants?

Opportunities for Growth

Does your company offer technical or soft-skill classroom training? Are there other, less formal means of learning in your company? Is one of your owners a guru who hosts brown-bag lunches with employees? Do you have technical experts from whom employees can acquire skills on the job? Since most organizations today are flat (offering little or no chance to move up), the opportunity to acquire skills and knowledge at work is very significant. As with benefits, make a list of these growth opportunities.

Assessing Your Company's Package

Armed with your great-place-to-work survey, benefits list, and growth opportunities list, you should be able to determine exactly what it is you have to offer—your company's package.

Now, ask yourself, is it a package that will attract the right applicants? Or does it need some work?

First, review the results of your workforce survey to determine what employees find most and least desirable about their jobs and workplace. Ask the following questions:

- What comes up most often in the "desirable" category?
- Is this an advantage over other organizations in your community?
- Are you currently using this in your recruitment advertising?
- What about the "least desirable" category? What answers appear here?
- Can you change the undesirables?

If there are several areas you'd like to change, prioritize them in terms of your company's business objectives and Hewitt's top ten list and develop a plan of action to address them.

Next, look at your benefits list and growth opportunities list. Ask the following questions:

- How do these stack up in terms of the top ten list? Highlight those that help employees in terms of their needs, fears, and goals.
- How can you build what you offer into your recruitment efforts?
- What's missing? If you need to make changes, for example, if your growth opportunities list is too short, investigate ways you can create these important opportunities in your organization.

Tailoring Your Package

The strength of your benefits package may depend on the target applicant. Employees with young children will be attracted to benefits like child care, flex time, and medical plans. Retirement plans and 401(k) options are popular with middle-aged workers. Older workers will be interested in medical plans and flexible hours.

No matter what their age or lifestyle, everyone is attracted to a place of work where they can make a difference, take pride in what they're doing, and enjoy the people they work with. The "great place to work" message should be a common thread in all your recruiting messages.

Choosing the Right Vehicle for Your Message

Now that you've defined what it is you have to offer (your package), it's time to plan the marketing of your package. By *marketing,* we mean all the communications your company will use to influence people to work for your company. Effective recruiting requires unconventional marketing methods—and sound strategy.

There is a myriad of marketing methods available to you; one can be just as good (or bad) as the next, depending on the situation. Therefore, your marketing plan should be guided by some strategic planning. Here are some suggestions:

> **Target Your Ads**
>
> Whenever you're considering any mode of communication to recruit candidates, ask yourself, "How likely is it that this mode will reach people with the competencies necessary for effective job performance?"

- **Examine the labor market within a 50-mile radius of your facility.** Study issues such as unemployment rates, competition for applicants, availability of skilled labor, and local downsizings. (Your local economic development board or state agencies can help you gather this information.) The intelligence you gather will give you a good idea about how difficult it will be to get qualified applicants into the "pool."

- **Consider new sources of labor.** Groups you target might include seniors (those 55 and over), homemakers reentering the workforce, people who are retiring or leaving the military or otherwise changing careers, and the economically disadvantaged. When communicating to such groups, remember to tailor your message to appeal to their situation. For example, individuals making a career change will be attracted to an advertisement that says "little or no training necessary."

- **Create an image.** Consider the specifics of what you want to communicate about your company and how you want it to be perceived in the community. Start developing a list of what you have to offer the community as well as your future employees.
- **Prepare a timeline and budget.** Establish a schedule and funding to kick off your recruitment efforts and begin developing an applicant pool.

Once you've done the preliminary work, you can start to think about the marketing techniques that will get your message to your target audience. Some of the more conventional, and unconventional, methods are described below.

Advertising

Advertising is an "umbrella" term that covers much more than the classified section in your local newspaper. Advertising costs your company money, but it gives you control over the message, the medium, and the timing. Various forms of advertising are discussed in the following section.

Newspapers. By far the most popular way to advertise job openings, newspapers are not always the most effective. Many of the best potential applicants may already be employed, so they aren't likely to be combing the help-wanted section of their local newspapers. They may, however, be looking at the sports section or lifestyle section of a newspaper. Place an ad in the section of the paper where your target audience is most likely to see it. Your local newspaper-advertising represen-

> **Class-Up Your Classifieds**
>
> **TRICKS OF THE TRADE**
>
> If you use classified ads in your advertising campaign, make them interesting, upbeat, and large enough to be seen. Write the copy to highlight what an applicant would find most attractive about the job—especially an applicant who already has another job. For example, if you pay well, provide great benefits, offer flex time, or have an on-site day-care facility, advertise it!

tative will be able to provide you with information on the demographics of readers.

Newsletters. Local colleges and universities, trade or technical schools, special-interest groups for hobbies like fishing or golf, and even churches often sell advertising in their newsletters. These types of publications may not boast big circulation figures, but they can be an effective way to reach your target audience. Again, check to make sure the readership profile matches the persons you want to reach.

Employment Publications. These regional newspapers and magazines are usually distributed weekly to high-traffic retail locations, outdoor distribution boxes, public libraries, career centers at high schools, technical and vocational schools, and colleges. Advertising in employment publications is often less expensive than placing classified ads in newspapers. You can get more space for less money, but your exposure is limited to people who read such publications.

Radio. Radio provides an opportunity to zero in on your audience because each station has a very specific audience in terms of age, gender, and income. Each station can provide you with information about the demographics of their listeners. Radio is especially effective at reaching people with a message about work opportunities while they're at work or on their way to work. Consider these facts: 61% of adults have a radio at work; radio listening dominates media usage at work, greater than TV, newspapers, and magazines combined; and 87% of adults

Do Radio Right

While the cost of running a single, 60-second radio spot may not seem very high, you need a lot of them to make an impression. For example, running 20 spots during morning drive time at $200 a shot adds up to $4,000! If you're going to invest in radio spots, be sure you give the listener a chance to write down the necessary information. If you mention a phone number or address in the ad, repeat it. In fact, you should repeat it five or ten times! This may seem like overkill, but it works.

who commute to work go by car, with the radio on 97% of the time. Running a single, 60-second radio spot (on popular radio stations) costs about $200 during morning drive time, midday, and afternoon hours; evening spots usually run about $50; and it'll cost you only $25 to run an ad during "graveyard" hours (because there are fewer listeners at these times).

Direct Mail. Consider buying a targeted list of individuals who match the profile of your recruits. Responder lists—even though they cost more—are best. These are lists of people whose responses to solicitations for service or merchandise indicate certain interests. For example, if you need to hire a human resources director, you might buy a list of people who attended a human resources conference sponsored by SHRM (Society for Human Resource Management) or the American Management Association. If you need to hire salespeople, buy a list of participants who attended a Miller Heiman's Strategic Selling seminar. Ask persons in your organization to provide you with the names and numbers of associations that are relevant to the particular position you are recruiting for. When you call an association, ask for the marketing or member services department. These are usually the departments that manage the mailing lists for these associations.

Job Fairs. Where else can you see hundreds of potential job applicants in just one day? Job fairs sponsored by local colleges, technical schools, and even radio stations often draw applicants from a wide geographical area. Some organizations even conduct their own job fairs or participate in virtual job fairs via Internet job search sites. If you recruit nationally, you might participate in job fairs in areas where large companies are downsizing.

Because you get only a few minutes with each

Know Your Job Fair

Before signing up for a job fair, talk to the sponsor. Find out how many companies are participating, how many job seekers typically attend and their demographics, how many years the job fair has been in existence, and the cost. Ask for company names as well as the names of individuals who have participated, and call to find out what kind of results they got.

TRICKS OF THE TRADE

applicant, be prepared. Know what you're looking for in a résumé (e.g., education, work experience) so you can screen résumés quickly. Ask questions that will give you insights into the applicant's competence and fit with the job. (Why are you leaving your current job? Why are you interested in working for our organization? What do you like best about your most recent job? What do you consider to be your greatest achievement at work?)

Job fairs are also a time when applicants are getting a first impression of your company. Make it a good one. Use displays or product demonstrations (great for drawing a crowd at your booth) that communicate loud and clear that your company is a great place to work. Handing out marketing materials—pamphlets, pens, etc.—can also help leave a more lasting, positive impression.

Internet. At least three Internet recruiting surveys conducted during 1997 (Olsten, JWT Communications, and Austin Knight) agreed in their conclusions that the number of key hires is small but growing and that companies are accelerating plans to use the Internet for staffing. According to the surveys, 17% to 67% of companies have used the Internet for recruiting.

If your company has a Web site, check and see if there's a place to list job openings. If not, find out how it can be added (directly to the site or through a link). It is a great way to advertise career opportunities with your company.

CAUTION!

Not Everyone's on the 'Net

Certain groups of people are going to have computer access while others are less likely to. You may find that applicants for certain positions are less likely to have Internet access. You may be overlooking a large portion of your potential applicant pool if you restrict your recruiting to the Internet.

There are numerous national Internet job search sites that offer a variety of services and information for employers and job seekers. Table 3-1 lists some of the current, more popular national sites. Searching these job sites is usually free to the job seeker.

SITE NAME	INTERNET ADDRESS
The Internet Job Searcher	http://www.joblocator.com/jobs/
America's Job Bank	http://www.ajb.dni.us/index.html
Best Jobs in USA	http://bestjobsusa.com/
Career Magazine	http://www.careermag.com/careermag/
Career Mosaic	http://www.careermosaic.com
Career Web	http://cweb.com/
CareerPath	http://careerpath.com/
E-Span	http://www.espan.com/
Jobnet	http://www.jobnet.com/
Jobtrak	http://www.jobtrak.com
JobWeb	http://www.jobweb.com
Wanted Jobs 98	http://www.wantedjobs.com
Monster Board	http://www.monster.com

Table 3-1. Internet sites for recruiting job candidates

When you get to the home page for these job search sites, there is usually a "hot button" called "Employers" that will link you to advertising options and rates. Options may include job postings, impact ads, and employer profiles:

- Job postings are basically electronic classified ads, which can be run for as little as $150 for two months. Some sites offer unlimited run time for this price (i.e., the ad runs until you're done hiring for that job).
- Impact ads are more dynamic and eye-catching (like the one used by Gore in our earlier example). They usually run for several months or longer and can cost substantially more than regular job postings.
- An employer profile is basically a home page that describes the company and that can be linked to all current job openings available at that company. These can cost several thousand dollars or more.

Options and rates vary, so be sure to check out what each site has to offer.

Professional associations will also post jobs related to their industry on their Web sites. Poll your employees to identify all professional associations relevant to your organization, and then contact those groups to post appropriate job openings or link their sites to yours.

One of the newest twists to Internet recruiting is the partnering with telecommunications companies and software companies to offer PC-to-PC interviewing. For example, recently recruiters from a large computer company in Texas conducted 25 interviews at an information technology trade show in New York without leaving their offices.

To zero in on the best Internet sites for local recruiting, check with your state economic development office. Many states have sites that link to specific counties. National recruiters with local offices and chambers of commerce may also help you locate Web sites for local recruiting.

Recruiting Agencies. These organizations include employment agencies, executive search firms, recruitment advertising agencies, and public job services. All can help you find and hire employees. All have advantages and disadvantages. The main advantage is the time they can save you. The main disadvantages are the cost and the quality of candidates they provide.

In dealing with any type of agency like this, remember that their mission is different from yours. Their mission is to get you to hire someone—*anyone*. That's how professional agencies make their money and how public job service agencies justify the need for their services and get people off their unemployment rolls. Your mission is to hire the most qualified applicant.

Choose agencies carefully. Find out what recruitment methods they use. Get references. Talk to other companies that have used them. Use them to help you obtain applicants, but not to make critical decisions about job requirements— and certainly not to make final hiring decisions.

Miscellaneous. Think of places where your potential applicants gather, then get creative with your messages. If you're
targeting people over 50, place posters at retirement-planning
seminars. Or buy space on handouts used at the workshop.
Billboards, public transportation, airports, and other public
places that allow advertising may also be effective in recruiting candidates. As with all other forms of advertising, investigate audience demographics and costs.

Public Relations

Public relations is the second major category heading for marketing strategies. While public relations activities are "free,"
they are "hit or miss." It is up to the editorial staff of a particular media outlet to run a story or not. And it's also up to them
(if they do run your story) to determine what to leave in and
what to leave out. Editors also control when and where the
information will appear. Let's take a closer look at some public relations strategies.

**Build Relationships with
Local Media.** Ask the
chamber of commerce to
supply you with a list of
print and broadcast media
serving a 50-mile radius
of your facility. With
newspapers, you'll want
to introduce yourself to
the business or industry

> **PR Firms Know the
> Media**   Smart
> Managing
> One advantage of using a
> local public relations firm is that it has
> established media relationships. For
> information on local public relations
> firms, contact the Public Relations
> Society of America at (212) 995-2230.

editors. For broadcast media, contact news directors or
assignment editors. If your organization does not have a public
relations department or someone who can devote the time to
developing relationships with the local press, you may want to
hire a public relations firm.

Showcase Events. Think of events that will be of interest to
the local community, and get this information to editors and
program directors. This type of information should go out in
the form of press releases every 30 days. Include the name of

a person they can contact to provide more information or to answer questions. Events may include:
- New products
- New jobs
- Community involvement
- Tax base increase
- Local suppliers used or hired by your company
- Improvements to local infrastructure

Appoint a Spokesperson. A spokesperson for your company should be knowledgeable, articulate, and accessible. It's wise to anticipate negative reactions to what seems to be positive news. Prepare statements concerning any potentially negative issues in advance.

Recruit at Schools. Visit with faculty and administrators at both the high school and college levels and develop a relationship with these professionals. Many students turn to them for advice on careers, so make sure they're aware of the job opportunities with your company. Find out about their cooperative education and internship programs. These can give you the edge in getting fresh talent in your door. Also investigate events such as lectures and job and career fairs that you can participate in. Ask about when you can schedule on-campus recruiting with the placement office. As discussed earlier, use student newspapers, newsletters, or radio to promote your presence. Place posters all around campus to tell when and where you'll be recruiting.

Speak Out. Check with the chamber of commerce and appropriate government agencies, such as the economic development board, about local speaking opportunities. These opportunities may range from a keynote address at a professional organization to an informal career day presentation at a local school.

Sponsor Community Events. Ask local officials if there are events in the community that require sponsorship. Then, select events that attract the type of people you're seeking. Don't just give your money. Give of yourself by volunteering, and get twice the exposure plus a feeling of community pride.

You may also want to consider participating in goodwill operations such as soup kitchens or the Salvation Army. These promote your organization as a positive force in the community.

Summary of Recruiting Methods

As you can see, there are many ways to market your company and its available positions. While you probably won't need to use all of the methods discussed in this chapter, we suggest you choose at least a couple from both the advertising and public relations sections and use them to expand your sources for applicants. Remember: you can hire only the people who apply. Getting the word out to as many qualified applicants as possible will increase your ability to hire the best possible people for your jobs.

Evaluating Your Recruiting Efforts

Once you've spent time and money on recruiting, wouldn't it be nice to know if your efforts paid off?

Actually, it would be more than just "nice." Evaluating the success of your recruiting methods will provide valuable information that can be used to improve your efforts.

One way to do this is to have a place on your application

Let Them Know How to Apply

Whatever methods of communication you use, make it clear how to apply for work at your organization. Do they mail or fax a résumé? If so, where? Do they stop by and fill out an application? When and where do they need to go? Do they call for an appointment?

Make sure that whoever will be greeting applicants or accepting calls or applications knows what to do and is helpful to the applicant. Nothing makes a worse first impression on an applicant than a company representative who is unaware that you're hiring for a particular position or who acts indifferent and isn't helpful. When people respond to your recruiting efforts, you have a prime opportunity to show them that your company is a great place to work.

where applicants can tell you where they heard about the job and your company. (If you use résumés instead of applications, the source is often included in a candidate's cover letter.) This is a great choice when you have a lot of applicants for a large number of positions. The information can be stored in your applicant tracking system. (See Chapter 5 for more information on applicant tracking.) Then, you can look at the successful applicants (i.e., those who passed various stages of your selection process) and see which recruiting methods attracted them to your company.

Alternatively, if you have a small applicant pool and only a few jobs to fill, you could use a less formal method of evaluation. For instance, in your screening interview you can ask candidates where they heard about you. Or, you can ask only those that you hired. (After all, these are the kind of people you want to attract with your recruiting efforts!)

Manager's Checklist for Chapter 3

❑ Make sure your organization is a great place to work. Part of doing that is having innovative recruiting processes.

❑ In convincing the best people to join your organization, benefits that are consistent with employee needs are important, but not the most important concern.

❑ Recruiting involves marketing. Know your geographic market, then use a mix of media to get your recruiting message out to those you want to apply.

❑ Media to consider when recruiting include newspapers, newsletters, regional employment magazines, direct mail, radio, job fairs, and the Internet. A public relations firm can help you get your message out as well.

❑ Evaluate your recruiting methods to see if you're getting the results you want.

Applications as Screening Tools

B usiness was booming, and Arthur Industries was expanding. In support of the expansion project, Arthur Industries advertised openings for skilled maintenance technicians. Interested applicants were asked to pick up an application at their local employment agency. The response was great. By the end of the week, the expansion project manager at Arthur Industries was staring at a stack of applications 6 inches high!

As she perused the applications, an uneasy feeling began to settle in. Propping her weary head in her hands, she asked herself, "What do I do now? We need experienced millwrights. How am I supposed to figure out who has the technical skills we need from this generic company application? We can't possibly test everyone in this stack!"

What happened?

Arthur Industries was not fully prepared. The company knew what technical skills were needed and had tests to assess them. However, Arthur Industries didn't realize that an application can be another assessment tool. By using the generic application that applied to all hourly positions (from laborers to clerical staff), the company missed a critical opportunity to gather important information up front about its applicants. That information would have saved the hiring manager a lot of guesswork and valuable time and test resources.

Does this sound familiar? Ironically, applications are the most widely used and most frequently misused means of assessment. Many organizations do not think of applications as assessment tools. However, if used properly, they can be effective.

In this chapter, you'll learn about the following topics:

- Using applications, résumés, or both
- How to develop a good application
- Screening applications
- Tracking applicant information
- Using automated technology

Using Applications, Résumés, or Both

Generally speaking, applications tend to be more suitable (and hence more common) for hourly or entry-level jobs, whereas résumés tend to be more suitable for professional or managerial positions. However, nothing says it has to be that way. Applications are acceptable tools for obtaining structured information from all applicants for any position. Also, with increasing access to computers and word processors, résumés are becoming more common among applicants for hourly positions as well.

Applications and résumés serve the same objective—to collect information about people interested in positions with your company. However, each approach has benefits as well as potential drawbacks. Let's take a closer look at each.

Applications

The big advantage of applications is that they're structured and straightforward. Their fill-in-the-blank format makes them easy for applicants to complete. Applications require the applicant to provide information the company wants to know (which limits omissions) and do not offer a lot of room for the applicant to furnish information the company doesn't need to know (which limits embellishment). For these reasons, they are relatively easy for reviewers to evaluate. You'll really appreciate this aspect if you have a lot of applicant responses to sort through!

On the flip side, the close-ended format of applications limits creativity, which can be a drawback if you're hiring for certain types of jobs (e.g., graphic designer). Another potential disadvantage is the cost associated with developing and distributing applications.

Résumés

Résumés allow applicants much greater freedom. This may be an advantage for you if you're interested in creativity or written communication skills. But the format makes résumés more difficult to evaluate, as each applicant will choose to include different information. Applicants are free to cover or emphasize what they feel is important (e.g., "studied at Yale") and to omit information that they do not want you to know (e.g., "flunked out of Yale"). They may also put down information that you unexpectedly find useful. For example, they may mention that they do not like to travel, when your position requires travel 50% of the time, or they may not list a college degree, when your position requires one. You can gain information that may help you make your initial screening decisions. Another positive aspect of résumés is that technology has made writing and distributing résumés faster and easier. This is great when you are swamped and need to hire someone by yesterday! (We'll tell you how to screen résumés in the next chapter.)

The pros and cons of applications and résumés are summarized in Table 4-1.

If you're still having trouble deciding between a résumé and an application, the good news is that you don't have to choose. In some instances, it makes sense to use them together, thereby reaping the benefits of each.

One option is to screen candidates via their résumés. After careful review, you can send formal applications to the most

	Applications	Résumés
Pros	• Straightforward • Structured • Limit embellishment • Easier to evaluate	• Open-ended; promote creativity • Allow applicants to emphasize what they feel is important • Allow applicants to "hang" themselves • Less expensive and easier to solicit
Cons	• Close-ended; limit creativity • More expensive to develop and distribute	• Allow applicants to omit information • Foster embellishment • Harder to evaluate

Table 4-1. The pros and cons of résumés versus applications

promising candidates. You may also want to include a supplemental questionnaire along with the application, to gather additional competency data. An example would be a questionnaire including instructions such as "Describe the most difficult challenge you faced at work, explain why it was the most challenging, and show how you approached the situation."

Using a résumé followed by an application allows you to learn more about your candidates—perhaps much more, if you include a supplemental questionnaire. It also helps shrink the applicant pool, because only the most seriously interested or motivated candidates will bother to complete and return the materials.

The key is to use the instrument(s) that will give you the most useful information, information that will help you make initial screening decisions. The job requirements will largely influence what information will prove to be useful. With either approach, you will need to have a clear picture of what the job requires in order to choose the right instrument and use it as an effective screening tool.

How to Develop a Good Application

Let's say you've decided to use an application as an initial screening tool. With the software and printing capabilities available today, there's no excuse for relying on a generic company application (or worse yet, a generic catalog version). Not only will you be missing out on valuable information, as in this chapter's opening example, but you may also be violating state regulatory laws.

By design, standard or generic applications are OK for most jobs but not great for any.

Take, for example, the standard company application that asks applicants how many words per minute they type, what software programs they know, and what office machines they are capable of running. Now ask yourself, "How does this apply to maintenance technicians?"

Sending Out Applications

If you follow up résumés with an application, it's a good idea to include a cover letter thanking applicants for their interest and congratulating them for making the first "cut." You may also want to take advantage of this opportunity to include some additional information about the position and the company. And, it helps if you include a self-addressed, stamped return envelope!

Using a generic application may seem like a cost- and time-effective option in the beginning. However, when you consider the lost productivity and the potential legal liability from using an inadequate application, the time and money saved up front become insignificant.

There's yet another reason to tailor your company's application. You've heard of the saying, "Image is everything." It applies here as well. An application is often the first impression a company gives an applicant. What does your application say about you? If it's more

Make Your Applications Legal

Often, applications are developed at corporate headquarters and may comply only with federal guidelines and those for that particular state. Before using any application, consult the Guideline to Pre-Employment Inquiries put out by the EEOC and your state's Fair Employment Practices Commission for more extensive regulatory application guidelines.

than ten years old or was developed for use in a different state, it's probably in dire need of an update. Before you panic at the thought of updating your application, take a look at the simple steps below that will guide you through developing a useful and cost-effective screening tool.

Step 1: Review Existing Applications

Applications have been around for a long time. We are not reinventing the wheel. Take a look at other applications. Note what you like and what you don't like about each of them.

Step 2: Select Those Items That Best Suit Your Needs

This is what tailoring is all about. Not every item on an application is suitable for every position. Choose those items that will provide you with the most useful screening criteria. Box 4-1 lists some basic elements to consider.

When deciding which items to choose, make sure you include questions that represent "knockout" factors. A knockout factor reflects a criterion that must be met in order to be considered for the job. For instance, if the job requires shift work and overtime, you should definitely include a question like, Do you have any commitments that would prevent you from working shifts or overtime? Applicants who indicate "Yes" to this item would be knocked out of the running. You can save a lot of time and money by screening for knockout factors in the beginning.

CAUTION!
Keep Them Consistent

One reason that older, more generic applications continue to be used is that the company has a database for information from those applications. When you design a new application, make sure you know where the information will be stored and, if necessary, how it can be translated into the existing database.

Step 3: Check the Application for Legality

Once you've chosen the items you want to include, review the content for legality. Does it comply with federal and state regulations? Table 4-2 (page 60) provides some help to get you started in this area.

Background information
- Contact information (phone, address)
- Social Security number
- Position applied for
- Salary expected
- When/how soon are you available?
- How did you learn about the position?
- Why do you want to work for us?
- Are you 19 years of age or older?
- Do you have a legal right to work in the United States?
- Have you ever applied to or worked for us under a different name?
- Have you been convicted of a crime in the past ten years? (If so, explain.)

Education and Training
- Names and addresses of educational institutions
- Did you graduate and with what degree?
- Where and when did you receive your GED?
- Military service (dates and places, branch, duties, rank, when discharged)

Work Experience
- Names and contact information for past employers, including type of business
- Position and job duties
- Dates of employment
- Name and title of supervisor
- If current employer, may we contact?
- Rate of pay (beginning and ending)
- Reason for leaving

Specific Job Requirements
- A technical skills or work experience checklist
- Any other skills or abilities we should know about (e.g., equipment that you can operate)?
- Would you be able to work any shift and/or overtime?
- Do you have a valid driver's license?
- Can you travel?

Other
- A list of professional references (don't bother asking for personal references)
- A statement granting authorization to verify the information, acknowledging that it is correct, and agreeing to submit to a drug test and medical examination as a condition of employment
- An "employment at will" statement (if applicable) stating that termination or resignation can occur with or without cause at any time

Box 4-1. Possible elements to include in an application

Topic Area	Don't Ask	Do Ask
Name	Have you ever worked under a different name?	Have you ever worked for this company under a different name?
Marital status/gender	Please check Mr., Mrs., Ms., or Miss	None
Gender	Male or female?	None
Age	How old are you? What is the date of your birth?	Are you 18 years of age or older?
Religion	What is your religious denomination or affiliation? What religious holidays do you observe?	None
Race or national origin	What is your race, nationality, or ancestry?	None
Photograph	Please affix a photograph to the application.	None
Citizenship	What country are you a citizen of? When did you acquire citizenship?	Do you have a legal right to work in the United States?
Language	What is your native language?	Do you write or speak any languages other than English?
Disability	Do you have a disability?	None
Education	When did you attend/ graduate?	What schools did you attend? Did you graduate?
Emergency notification	Whom should we notify in case of an emergency? What is their relationship to you?	None
Organizations	What organizations or clubs do you belong to?	What job-relevant organizations are you a member of? (Voluntary)

Table 4-2. Unlawful versus lawful application questions

In some instances, to comply with EEOC reporting standards, you may have to collect information about applicants' race, gender, age, and so on. Of course, this information cannot be used to make screening decisions. Therefore, we suggest developing a detachable section for collecting this data—detachable because this information should not be stored with the application. Make sure to state clearly that this information is for complying with federal reporting guidelines only, is strictly voluntary for the applicant to provide, and will not be a factor in employment consideration in any way.

Items to Include

Smart Managing

When selecting items to include on an application, keep in mind that some items do not necessarily help you screen applications, but will help you with other aspects of your selection system. Take for example the item, "How did you learn about the position?" While the responses to this item will not help you differentiate among applicants, they will help you evaluate the effectiveness of the applicant recruiting techniques you learned about in Chapter 3. Likewise, when it comes time to check references, it will be very helpful to know if it's OK to speak with the applicant's current employer. Thus, we suggest including an item like, "If currently employed, may we contact?"

Step 4: Format the Application Logically

Make the application simple and straightforward. Use common sense. If your application is difficult to complete, you may not get the information you want or applicants may decide not to fill it out at all. Also, be sure to allow enough space for responses. Applicants will provide only as much information as you allow them room to do so. Another formatting tip is to put the contact information and the basic knockout questions first. That way, when you need someone's phone number, it's right on top, and when you see that the forklift driver applicant does not have a driver's license, you don't have to waste your time scanning the rest of the application.

Step 5: Take One Last Look

It's always a good idea to take one last look at what you've got. For each item you plan to use, ask the following questions:

- Will this item likely get me the information I need?
- Is that information job-relevant?
- Will that information help me differentiate between qualified and less qualified applicants?

If the answer to any of the above questions (especially the last two) is "No," you should seriously question why you should include it. Using this test not only pays off in better hiring decisions but also limits your legal liability.

Screening Applications

Once the applications come pouring in, what do you do with them? Basically, what do you look for? Well, that depends on the job—or, as we learned in Chapter 1, the success profile for the job.

Before you review an application, you need to have a clear picture of the job requirements. Then you can create a checklist for screening the application. This is one of the most important steps in the process. If you fail to complete this step, your application will not be a useful screening tool.

The checklist should correspond to the items you have included in the application. For example, if applicants must be at least 18 years old to be employed by your company, their responses to that item should be included in your checklist. A comprehensive checklist will allow you to prioritize applications based on how closely they match your job profile(s). To keep things simple, we suggest that you prioritize applications using four bands (A to D).

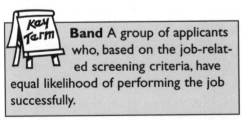

Band A group of applicants who, based on the job-related screening criteria, have equal likelihood of performing the job successfully.

Applicants in Band A are the closest match to the initial job profile. Band B represents the second-closest match, and

	A	B	C	D
18 years of age or older?	✔	✔	✔	
Legal right to work in U.S.?	✔	✔	✔	
Able to work any shift?	✔	✔	✔	
Convicted of a violent crime or theft?				✔
Has a valid, unsuspended driver's license?	✔	✔	✔	
Has a school diploma or equivalent?	✔	✔	✔	
Has 2-year technical skills degree or equivalent?	✔	✔		
Has 5 or more years of related work experience?	✔			
Has 2-4 years of related work experience?		✔		
Has PLC experience (maintenance electricians only)?	✔	✔		
Has millwright or fabricating experience (maintenance mechanics only)?	✔	✔		
Stable job history (not "job jumping")?	✔	✔		
No unexplained gaps in job history?	✔	✔		
Some risk factors in leaving jobs?			✔	
Substantial risk factors in leaving jobs?				✔
Unrealistic wage or salary expectations?			✔	✔
Did not sign application?				✔

Figure 4-1. Sample maintenance technician application screening checklist

Band C is third. Applicants in Band D do not meet the profile and will likely never proceed to testing or an interview. In other words, the criteria in Band D represent knockout factors, such as not having a legal right to work in the United States. Figure 4-1 depicts a sample application screening checklist for a maintenance technician position.

Prioritize applications as A, B, C, or D, based on the criteria listed in the left column. For example, to earn an A rating,

Don't Overlook Someone

As a quality control measure, it's useful to have someone spot-check the applications in Bands B and C to ensure that you don't overlook suitable candidates. You can also have someone other than the person responsible for interviewing and/or hiring conduct the initial screening. This tends to increase fairness and accuracy, as an individual's biases are less likely to influence the decision about a candidate.

an application must meet all the criteria checked in the A column. If it does not meet all the necessary criteria for A, look at each subsequent column until all the criteria are met. If it meets none of the minimum criteria for A, B, or C, a D rating is appropriate.

You must go through the entire checklist to determine the appropriate band for each application. Let's say there are ten items on the list and an application meets the criteria for Band A all the way through number nine. Then for item ten, the applicant's response falls into Band C. The application would receive a C. This may seem unfair at first; after all, the person met the Band A criteria in 90% of the categories. However, you need to keep in mind that the checklist was developed with this in mind. The goal is to be able to prioritize applications so you can call the most highly qualified people first. Each category on the checklist is an important screening criterion. Otherwise, it would not be on the list!

In addition to the screening checklist, there are a few other questions to ask:

- **Is the application filled in completely?** Or is valuable information missing? An application that is 50% complete is not really 50% useful. However, missing information (including applicant signature) may simply be an oversight. If you have enough information to make you think applicants are qualified for the job, call them and ask if they would come in to complete the application for further processing. Their response to this request will tell you how interested they are in working for your company.

- **Did the applicant understand and follow directions?** This could be a red flag if it happens more than once on an application. The applicant may have difficulty reading and/or following directions, which could be a concern for jobs that require these skills. On the other hand, the instructions could be misleading, especially if you see the same mistake on multiple applications.
- **Can you understand the information provided by the applicant?** Although grammar and spelling may not be an essential part of the position(s) you're trying to fill, the information has to be clear enough that you can accurately evaluate it.
- **Does the information check out?** In other words, do the dates of employment make sense and are the job responsibilities in line with the position the applicant listed? At this point, look for such things as unexplained gaps in work histories.

The outcomes of the above questions determine whether or not the information will be useful in your decision-making process. This is the key to it all. The application needs to give you enough relevant information to decide which applicants merit more of your time, energy, and resources for further evaluations.

Tracking Applicant Information

This section covers an often-overlooked part of screening applications—tracking the information. It's often overlooked, because it is seen as tedious. However, anyone who has had to process a significant number of applications can tell you how crucial a good tracking system is. Not only will you have important information at your fin-

> **Track 'Em**
>
> TRICKS OF THE TRADE
>
> Set up a logical, comprehensive applicant tracking system in the beginning. We guarantee you'll be glad you did! It will help you identify candidates who have the skills you're looking for when you're looking for them.

There's Got to Be a Better Way

A renowned automobile manufacturer announced plans for a new facility. In the first six months alone, the company received over 65,000 applications! Unfortunately, believe it or not, the only way the company knew that was by counting the number in one box, weighing it, and then weighing the rest of the boxes. The company neglected to design and use a good up-front applicant tracking process. Later, it wished it had—especially when it came to looking for applicants with specific skills.

gertips (such as how many people have applied in the past two weeks), but you will also be able to easily put together reports to comply with EEOC guidelines, if that should become necessary.

The time spent tracking and documenting people who apply to your company may seem like a waste, but consider the two examples described in the "For Example" boxes on this page.

An accurate applicant tracking system benefits every company—large or small. Of course, the number of applications you receive each month dictates how detailed or complex your tracking system needs to be. If the number is in the teens, you may need only a log of names and dates; you can

Three Is Too Many

A Fortune 500 company was looking for skilled technicians. Using many of the recruiting techniques outlined in Chapter 3, it had several hundred people fill out applications. One applicant filled out three of them. Because he had the requisite skills and experience, he made the initial cut and was called in for testing and interviewing—three times! Fortunately, one of the assessors recognized the candidate from an earlier visit. Although he did not pass on any of his three attempts (good thing the test was reliable!), it was a waste of time for both the company and the applicant. Moreover, that situation could have been easily prevented.

refer to the applications for more information. However, if the number is in the hundreds, you will need a much more comprehensive system. Figure 4-2 shows a page from a spreadsheet that includes the typical information needed in a more comprehensive system. Of course, the system is only as useful as the data you put into it. (Remember the adage "garbage in, garbage out"?) The trick to developing a

> ### Tracking Database
> The tools to develop a tracking system do not need to be complicated. You probably have what you need already installed on your computer in the form of Microsoft Excel or Access. These programs allow you to create databases and sort information about your applicants. Another advantage to using software spreadsheets and databases is that you can back up, store, and retrieve the information much more easily than with paper filing systems. Whatever tracking method you choose, we recommend keeping your records for at least one year.

good applicant tracking program is to ask yourself two questions:

- What do I need to know about the applicants who apply?
- What would anyone else—from the CEO to the EEOC—possibly want to know about our applicants?

The answers will probably lead you to creating a very useful tracking system for your needs.

Using Automated Technology

Of course, there are other, more advanced tools to help companies track applicant data and print reports. Much of this technology can help you screen applications and résumés.

Is this new technology right for you? It depends. If you're seriously considering automated technology, you'll need to consult a computer expert to find out about the latest software. But to get you started, we'll take a look at two broad categories of automation that may be useful in screening applications and résumés: front-end and back-end.

Last	First	SS#	Position	App Band	Assmt Date	Profile	Inter-view	Pass	Ref Chk	Offer Date	Wage	Drug Test	Pass	Hire Date	W/D	Comments
Apple	Ted	589214389	Maint	A	21 Jan	A	27 Jan	Yes	Pass	28 Jan	17.10	29 Jan	Yes	7 Feb		
Brown	Julius	789097654	Prod	B	22 Jan	B	27 Jan	Yes	Fail							poor attitude
Darwin	Guy	234129876	Prod	D												
Garcia	Tomas	476981234	Maint	A	21 Jan	B	28 Jan	Yes	Pass	30 Jan	17.10				Y	rejected offer
White	Latoya	129658743	Maint	B	No show											reschedule
Keeler	Susan	780537592	Qual	B	17 Jan	B	25 Jan	No								
Nye	Robert	962123579	Prod	C												
Olson	Ken	863391257	Prod	B	22 Jan	B	26 Jan	Yes	Pass	27 Jan	9.75	28 Jan	No			

Key to Column Headings: Last name, First name, Social Security number, Position applied for, Application screen band (A, B, C, or D), Date of assessment, Profile based on assessment scores (A, B, C), Date of final interview, Pass interview (yes or no), Outcome of reference check, Date of offer, Wage offered, Date of drug test, Outcome of drug test, Hire date, Withdrew (yes if applicant withdrew from process at any stage), Comments (explanations for any other category).

Figure 4-2. Typical spreadsheet for tracking applications

Front-end technology concerns the reception of applications. Some organizations that screen a lot of candidates have gone to "paperless" applications. As an alternative to the traditional forms, applicants fill in blanks via a computer terminal at a central location (e.g., a recruiting center) or over the Internet. In addition to reducing the "paper trail," this system offers the advantage of allowing company administrators to perform system queries, such as to check how many engineering candidates applied in the past week. Some organizations have used scannable bubble sheets (like the old achievement test forms) to collect information. These forms are then fed through a scanner to collect and record applicant data. Likewise, administrators can perform system queries using any of the fields included on the application.

Back-end technology concerns the screening of applications and résumés. More and more Fortune 500 companies (which typically receive large numbers of unsolicited résumés) are turning to software packages that scan documents according to programmed criteria. The software searches for those résumés that contain key words and phrases. The big advantage of this technology is that you do not waste your time wading through dozens of résumés to find candidates with a degree in electrical engineering. The software will do this for you. All you have to do is perform system queries to filter out the information of interest.

Finally, many Internet job search sites (such as those discussed in Chapter 3) offer services to employers that include receiving résumés electronically and screening them using keyword searches. Fees and the quality of service provided vary, so check into all of your options.

Sound too good to be true? Well, before you decide on jumping on the technology bandwagon, you need to consider the pros and cons listed in Table 4-3.

If the pros outweigh the cons, then investing in application screening technology may make sense for you. As technology changes and improves, we need to keep our eyes and ears

Benefits	Drawbacks
• It's fast. • It's more objective. It treats every résumé and application the same. • It automatically stores, sorts, and tracks applicant data, allowing quick retrieval of data and eliminating the need for cumbersome filing systems. • Fewer resources are needed to run it. • If you need computer-literate employees, the use of a front-end system allows you to screen out applicants who are afraid of using computers.	• It only does what you program it to do and doesn't make allowances for compensatory information. Suitable applicants may be screened out just because their résumés are missing key words. • Not everyone is comfortable using a computer. If this is the only application method you use, you may be missing out on or even discriminating against otherwise qualified applicants. • Automated systems are not foolproof. Applicants may know what back-end systems are programmed to look for and make sure those key terms are peppered throughout their résumés. • It can be quite expensive.

Table 4-3. The benefits and drawbacks of technology to screen applicants

open. New applications and breakthroughs are literally just round the corner. Given the importance of effective application and résumé screening, it would be wise to seriously consider any method that may improve the process.

No matter what method you use, the key point is to be systematic! By evaluating all candidates against the same screening standards, your process will be more objective, fair, and accurate.

Manager's Checklist for Chapter 4

❑ Determine what information you most need from your applicants. Then decide whether a résumé, an application, or both will best provide this information.

❑ When creating an application, be sure (1) knockout questions are included up front to screen out obviously inappropriate candidates, (2) all questions are legal and/or in
compliance with federal guidelines, (3) questions are presented in a simple, logical, easy-to-understand format.

❑ Create a checklist for reviewing applications that allows
you to prioritize the applications according to your criteria
for the knowledge, skills, abilities, and motivations
required for effective job performance.

❑ Stick to the checklist criteria when making decisions about
which band to place an applicant in and which applicants
to move forward in the process.

❑ Set up an applicant tracking system so that you can
retrieve relevant information from your applications quickly and efficiently.

❑ If you process a large number of applications, consider
investing in application screening technology.

❑ Whatever system you develop, do not become a slave to
it. If it's not working properly, modify it. If a high percentage of applicants make it through the initial screening but
then fail in subsequent stages of the selection process,
your screening criteria may be too lenient or your subsequent criteria may be too strict. Adjust your criteria as
necessary.

Screening
Résumés

"Percy, do you have a minute?" Sam asked as he leaned against Percy's office door. Sam was holding the second memo that he had received from Percy this week containing spelling and grammar errors. Thinking the first time was just a fluke, Sam had let it go. But now he was concerned that their customers were getting documents like this.

Percy rubbed his chin, thinking of what to say. "Well, Valerie, my new administrative assistant, typed them for me. I didn't really check them before they went out," he sheepishly admitted. "But I'm sure the errors were oversights brought on by the stress of trying to get the McGillicutty proposal out on time. Trust me. Valerie's top-notch. Just look at her résumé," Percy assured Sam, as he handed him the assistant's résumé.

What Sam saw was not reassuring—quite the contrary. "Geez, Percy, on her cover page alone she misspelled 'initiative' and omitted a word. Didn't you catch this?"

What happened?

Percy had not taken the time to adequately review Valerie's cover letter and résumé. Instead, Percy had just focused on the big picture items—such as where she worked last and what her responsibilities were. Percy thought he was a good judge of character and would catch any weaknesses during the interview. As a result, Percy had ignored a valuable piece of job-relevant information—one supplied by the applicant herself. For many positions, presenting a professional image via written documents is essential. An effective assessment process takes this into account.

In this chapter, you'll learn about the following issues:
- What a cover letter can tell you
- How to screen résumés
- Follow-up phone calls

What a Cover Letter Can Tell You

A résumé is usually accompanied by a cover letter. Don't treat that letter as just a formality. You can get valuable information from carefully reading a cover letter. For instance, applicants often include additional information about their backgrounds and interests as they apply specifically to your organization's particular needs. When evaluating a cover letter, pay attention to professionalism, originality, and overall impression.

Professionalism

A cover letter is a business letter, so it should be formatted as such. Check for all the elements that make up a good business letter. For example, check to see if the letter is properly addressed and closed. Is it addressed "To whom it may concern," "Dear so-and-so," or simply "Dear Sir"? Are there grammar, spelling, or other types of errors? Consider such oversights seriously when the position you're filling involves writing documents. Conscientious candidates will double- and triple-check to ensure accuracy. After all, this will be your first impression of them.

Originality

"Originality" doesn't mean that the cover letter plays a tune like "hire Chuck—he's no lame duck" when you open it. It means that the applicant tailored the letter to your company; it was not just one of 100 generic letters he or she sent out.

Originality shows commitment. An applicant who took the time to tailor a cover letter specifically for your company is probably motivated to secure employment with you. Moreover, if the applicant's comments demonstrate an understanding of your company and the position in question, that also says a lot. It is the rare applicant who actually researches the company he or she is applying to these days—especially when responding to every ad in the paper.

Overall Impression

Basically, did the applicant sell himself or herself to you? How did the cover letter impress you? Obviously, this factor is tremendously important for applicants seeking sales positions. However, each applicant should at least make a decent attempt at selling what he or she has to offer your company. This reflects competitive drive.

How to Screen Résumés

There are two basic types of résumés: chronological and experiential. The techniques described in this section can be applied to screening both types.

Chronological résumés are what most people picture when they think of résumés—and what employers usually prefer. As the name suggests, chronological résumés list employment history and experience in order of accomplishment. Because headings, dates, and responsibilities are usually clearly defined, chronological résumés are generally easier to review than experiential résumés.

However, the use of experiential résumés is on the rise. Many job search books recommend this type of

> **⚠ CAUTION!**
> **Screen Right**
> Your primary objective in screening candidates is to compare their initial profiles with your job-related requirements. Make sure you place the appropriate amount of emphasis on "stylistic" concerns, given the job responsibilities, but don't judge applicants too heavily on their ability to put together a fancy cover letter or résumé.

résumé, because the format allows for a more accurate profile of experiences and abilities than does a more traditional format.

Experiential résumés commonly list accomplishments and credentials (sometimes simply in the form of listed strengths) without reference to any employer. In other words, you may not have any clue as to where or how the candidate got the experience. Often, a list of employers appears at the end of the résumé. However, duties, titles, and even dates are commonly missing, which makes experiential résumés difficult to review. Whether or not the candidate used this format to hide information remains a question. Whatever the case, savvy résumé screeners must be aware of the possibility.

Differences in format make it harder to screen résumés than standardized applications. But, the screening criteria to use still depend on the job.

Tips for Screening Résumés

Before we get into specific screening criteria, here are some tips that you should keep in mind when reviewing résumés.
- Focus on job relevancy.
- Picture the job.
- Don't assume or jump to conclusions.
- Look for red flags.
- Ignore discriminatory information.
- Be reasonable.

Let's look at the details of each of these.

Job relevancy. Common sense dictates that you focus on what's relevant. What are the job requirements? What criteria are necessary for successful job performance? Look for key information like degrees and responsibilities. Also, take into consideration how similar and how recent the past positions were. For example, if you're filling a sales position, it would probably be beneficial for an applicant to have worked in a position involving sales, but less beneficial if many years have passed since the last sales position.

Picture the job. This goes beyond basic job requirements. How well would the applicant fit the position in terms of personality and motivation? Visualize what the person will be doing. Visualize who he or she will be working with. Visualize the work setting and the company culture. For example, if the position is in a team environment and the applicant has never worked in that type of culture, he or she might be less suitable than an applicant who has experience working in teams.

Don't assume or jump to conclusions. This is a common pitfall. Applicants are often vague on their résumés or purposefully misleading. Just because Ann mentions that she attended the University of Chicago and lists relevant courses, don't assume that she graduated unless it's clearly stated. Don't assume because Susan was club president that she also has leadership qualities—it may have been a very small club! Steven was a member of the soccer team and participated in intramural softball, but don't assume that he's a team player— he may have been a "hot dog" or a big whiner.

Look for red flags. Be alert to warning signals that things on a résumé may not be as they appear. For instance, a lack of dates and company specifics may indicate that the candidate is trying to hide something. Vague duty listings or overuse of hedgers or qualifiers may be an attempt to compensate for poor work experience. An emphasis on tangential matters such as hobbies and interests may also indicate weak work experience or job skills.

Ignore discriminatory information. Treat very carefully any information that could result in discrimination or charges of unlawful discrimination, such as age or number of children. In other words, ignore it! Refer to Chapter 2 on legal issues for more specifics on the type of information that could be considered discriminatory. If possible, we suggest crossing it out immediately. Check company policies before doing this, however. If you do not have a policy that covers discriminatory information, you may want to institute one.

Be reasonable. In other words, be flexible. For example, just because you do not like the color of the paper or the font the applicant used or you think ant farming is a stupid hobby, don't use this as a reason to screen out an otherwise qualified applicant. This goes along with our recommendation to focus on job relevancy.

These tips will help you distinguish useful information from not-so-useful information. Since single-page résumés are no longer the norm, you will appreciate being able to spot what's relevant and what's not.

Résumé Screening Checklist

The next thing you need to know is what should be included on the résumé screening checklist. Essentially, what are you really looking for? There are six factors that should be included in any résumé screening checklist:
- Overall appearance
- Layout
- Experience
- Education and credentials
- Relevant affiliations and activities
- References

The importance you give to each factor will depend on the nature of the job and the job requirements.

Overall Appearance. Is the résumé neatly written and legible? (Make allowances for legibility of faxed résumés.) Are there spelling or grammar mistakes? Is the paper of good quality? Is the content customized to your needs? True, some of these factors may seem trivial, but they provide insight into the care taken by the applicant and thus possibly his or her interest and motivation. A conscientious applicant will attend to such details. And, for some positions, such as that of newsletter editor, spelling and grammar errors are bona-fide knockout factors!

Layout. Is the résumé organized logically? Or does it skip around? Is it clear? Can you easily find what you're looking for? These characteristics are important for any résumé, but especially for chronological résumés. In addition, are the most important aspects listed first? For example, if the applicant has ten years of relevant job experience, is that listed before the educational or any personal data? Résumés that empha-

Résumés Can Fool You

Keep in mind that many candidates have someone or some agency help them prepare their résumé. Your initial impression may not be an accurate reflection of the applicant.

size education, clubs, honors, and hobbies over work history may indicate that the applicant is trying to compensate for weak work experiences. Last, is the format appropriate? In other words, is the format consistent throughout? Or does the applicant switch from italics to bold-face, from paragraphs to bullet points without reason? Is the style (i.e., fonts and typeface) creative and eye-catching? Or is it distracting? These factors show care and creativity.

Experience. This is the heart of the matter! Is the career progression logical? In other words, did the applicant progress to seemingly better positions and/or companies? Look for depth and watch for "job jumping" (i.e., a lot of jobs in a short period of time). Is position tenure appropriate? This is a tricky question. Long tenure with a company may indicate loyalty and proven value to the company, but it may also indicate a lack of risk taking and potential. Likewise, frequent "job jumps" may indicate assertiveness and high-potential (i.e., a "high flier")—or that the applicant is unable or unwilling to adapt, gets bored easily, or is a poor team player.

The most important aspects of work experience relate to job functions. Are the duties and tasks clear? In other words, do you understand what the applicant was responsible for? Are parameters clearly defined? Do not depend on job titles for this information. For instance, nothing is more vague than the title of "manager"!

To determine what the applicant has actually done, look for concrete terms such as "accomplished," "implemented," "used," and "supervised" and specifics such as "covered a three-state sales territory," "managed a $100,000 budget," or "supervised 15 employees." Concrete and specific information help make the résumé screening process more objective.

Does the résumé list accomplishments and achievements? Look for such things as "exceeded sales goal by 25%," "received award for developing a cost-saving innovation," or "implemented a new training program

> ### Vague Phrases
> Be wary of vague terms like "involved with," "helped," "suggested," "oversaw," "familiar with," "have knowledge of," or "envisioned." These phrases tell you nothing about what the applicant has actually done.

that reduced customer complaints by 15% in its first year." These indicators of success provide insight into what impact the applicant had on the bottom line.

Education and Other Credentials. Does the applicant's level of education match your requirements? In other words, common sense dictates that you would not want to hire someone with a four-year degree in the culinary arts to be your accountant. By the same token, you probably would not want to hire a new M.B.A. to be your administrative assistant—unless you don't mind replacing people every six months!

Does the applicant actually state that he or she graduated (and with what degree)? Or does the résumé just say "attended"? Although a college or a technical degree doesn't guarantee that the graduate has the appropriate skill or knowledge for the job, it does indicate that

> ### Be Careful of Ivy
> Do not be overly swayed by prestigious colleges or degrees. Although graduating from Harvard may say more about someone's potential than graduating from Eastern State U., do not let it inordinately influence your decision. The great majority of American CEO's don't have Ivy League backgrounds.

he or she was able to complete something. Does the applicant have the necessary licenses or training to be successful? Some positions (mostly technical or professional) require special certification, such as a CPA for an accountant. The trick here is not to screen out those who may be lacking certain training if those skills are easily taught on the job, such as CPR for a firefighter.

Relevant Affiliations and Activities. If an applicant furnishes this information, it may provide insights into his or her fit for the job. Again, the key is *relevancy*. Professional affiliations are generally the most helpful information. Current affiliations may reflect the applicant's interest in continuous learning and keeping abreast of new trends in his or her field. Activities listed may also help you assess the applicant. For example, somebody who volunteers in United Way activities and at the local food bank may be well suited for a position in social work. In general, however, most activities are not relevant; ignore them or at least don't give them much weight.

References. Are references included, along with contact information? Often, applicants will simply state, "references available upon request." This is common and acceptable. However, if they include letters of recommendation or accommodation, these documents can provide insight into what others thought of the applicant. (Note: You should still conduct a thorough reference check, as we will cover in Chapter 10.)

As you're reviewing résumés based on the factors described above, you may want to make a list of what impresses you about each résumé—both positively and negatively. This list can be used in making follow-up phone calls to the candidates.

Once you've screened the résumés, you can use a banding system like the one we suggested in Chapter 4 for screening applications. The applicants who match the criteria most closely would be in Band A, the next best in Band B, and so forth. Next, it may be helpful to add one more level to the résumé screening process—a follow-up telephone call to those in Band A (and possibly B and C bands, depending on the number and quality of résumés received).

Follow-up Phone Calls

Because résumés are less structured than applications, it's often necessary or at least wise to make a telephone call to

Preventive Note Taking

We recommend that you make your notes on a separate paper, rather than on the résumé.

Whatever you would write on the résumé might be seen by others (both inside and outside your organization)—and they could interpret comments much differently.

For example, after an interview you may want to jot down some notes to keep track of who's who. Noting certain characteristics (such as "older white guy with bad hair," "young Hispanic woman in blue suit," or "black man wearing union cap") may seem like an easy and innocent method to keep track of the applicants. However, that practice may not appear innocent to someone else (like the EEOC)—especially if the applicant files a grievance. This is a safe and simple policy that we recommend for résumés and for applications.

collect additional information. If you do this properly, you can accomplish four purposes.

1. **Provide a realistic job preview (RJP).** You can describe the position and your company in more detail. This should be a realistic job preview. This is a good way to see if the candidate is still interested in the position. While you should describe the work

Realistic job preview (RJP) This covers the benefits and potential drawbacks of a position. Make sure that it is, indeed, realistic.

environment and the position responsibilities, it is wise not to describe the characteristics or competencies you are looking for in a candidate. If you let them know what you are looking for, you can bet they will tell you exactly what you want to hear!

2. **Fill in the gaps.** You can collect additional information about responsibilities and accomplishments. For example, you may be interested in finding out exactly how the candidate reduced customer complaints by 15%. Was it through dedicated service? Or did business drop off so much that there were just fewer customers to complain?

Or you might be interested in finding out just what the applicant was doing during that two-year gap in his or her job history. Raising a family or going to school? Or spending time in one of our finer correctional institutions?

3. **Look at qualifications.** You can ask selected standardized questions to get at motivational fit (see Chapter 8) and other critical competencies. Use the results of your competency analysis to develop good interview questions.

Candidate: _____ Interviewer:_____ Date:_____

- Ask if this is a good time to talk. Explain purpose of interview.
- Describe organization and position.
- Provide a realistic job preview.
- Ask questions about work history.
- Clarify responsibilities by collecting specific examples.
- Fill in any gaps in work history.
- Ask what they liked most about their position(s).
- Ask what they liked least about their position(s).
- What do they consider their greatest work accomplishment?
- Investigate reasons for leaving companies and positions.
- Ask about career goals.
- Ask how they see this position fitting with those goals.
- Allow candidate to ask questions about company and position.
- Ask any follow-up questions.
- Close the interview.
- Thank the candidate for his or her time.

Note your rating, paying particular attention to person-job fit: **A   B   C   D**

Progress to next stage?   Yes   No

Comments:

Figure 5-1. A format for conducting a telephone screening interview

4. **Answer questions.** You can give the candidate a chance to ask questions about the position and the company. This approach can yield particularly useful information. A motivated and intelligent candidate will almost always have a few good questions to ask. You should be prepared to respond to questions concerning promotional opportunities, performance expectations, and compensation.

Figure 5-1 on the previous page outlines a format, along with some good questions to ask during a typical telephone screening interview.

Manager's Checklist for Chapter 5

❑ Read and evaluate the cover letter, placing the right amount of emphasis on it, in terms of the job requirements and responsibilities.

❑ Review any material accompanying the résumé (e.g., letters of accommodation). Use it as a springboard when you do your reference checks (see Chapter 10).

❑ Evaluate overall appearance, layout, experience, education, credentials, and relevant affiliations. Always emphasize the experience and place an appropriate amount of emphasis on the rest, according to the job requirements and responsibilities.

❑ If you'll be using a phone screen to follow up on résumés, develop a structured format. Allow time to touch on each of the four reasons for conducting a phone screen.

Interviewing Basics

Eric couldn't believe he was being interviewed by a man who had just run into the room eating a pastrami sandwich. As he sat trying to decide if the interviewer was purposely using his résumé for a place mat, he recalled the events that led up to the meeting and contemplated his next move.

A week earlier, Eric had participated in a phone screen and was asked to show up at 2 p.m. Thursday for a face-to-face interview. Yes! An interview with GXI Technology, one of *Fortune's* ten best companies to work for. The day of the interview he put on his best suit, grabbed his list of questions, and headed off for an interview with destiny. Unfortunately, destiny turned out to be an unprepared, overworked manager named Jim Pliers.

First, Jim shows up 30 minutes late. Eric figures, hey, it happens. This is GXI. People are busy here. Next, Jim is munching on a sandwich. Between bites, he asks Eric questions about where he's currently working and where he went to school. In less than two minutes, Eric realizes that Jim hasn't read his résumé. For the next 60 minutes, Jim seems to be ad-libbing questions, while Eric ponders how he ended up in an interview with the real-life version of Mr. Magoo.

What happened?

Welcome to the sadly all-too-common world of the ineffective interview. Eric is a star performer in his current company and could have been one for GXI. What prevented Jim from assessing Eric's true potential? What prevented Eric from discovering why GXI is one of *Fortune's* ten best companies? How much money did GXI lose by missing the opportunity to hire a top performer?

The fact is that you cannot underestimate the value of a well-conducted interview for choosing the right candidate and convincing the right candidate to choose you.

This chapter will help in preparing for such an interview and addresses the following topics:
- The cost of ineffective interviewing
- Five practical purposes for an interview
- Why traditional interviews don't work
- Avoiding interview bias
- Competency-based interviewing
- Structured interviewing

The Cost of Ineffective Interviewing

The interview is the most widely used and most misunderstood hiring technique. Every company uses some form of interviewing before making a hiring decision. Unfortunately, for all the time and effort spent interviewing, the result is generally not much better than a coin toss. Many times, the best candidate walks away, while the "What could we have been thinking?" candidate starts work on Monday.

The problem is that most interviewers believe they have been blessed with a supernatural ability to "read" people. Sure, there may be a few interviewers out there who can tell if candidates will make good employees by the firmness of their handshake, the way they sit during the interview, or their general approach to conversation. But the rest of us mere mortals need help to improve our chances of selecting the right candidate and having the right candidate select us.

OK, so what's the big deal if you don't always hire a qualified candidate? It has been estimated that the cost to a company for a supervisor making $30,000 a year is $470,000 over a ten-year period. So, the big deal can easily amount to over a million dollars if a company makes just two bad management hires over a ten-year period. Such astounding costs do not apply only to managerial positions. The average cost to hire at the professional level is $5,000 and an hourly employee in a production facility costs $1,600. When you consider recruiting, interviewing time, moving expenses, pay, benefits, and lost productivity, the numbers become staggering.

Not every poor hiring decision can be blamed on poor interviewing skills. But many can. Think about it. Interviewing is the most commonly used selection tool. The final decision about whether or not to hire a candidate usually rests on the outcome of the "final interview." Most hiring managers bank on the interview as being one of the best predictors of how well the person will perform on the job. And it should be. Unfortunately, it often is not.

The good news is that there are proven interviewing techniques that you can use today to help you better predict a candidate's performance tomorrow. After more than a decade of doing research and training interviewers, we've found the techniques outlined in this chapter have the greatest impact for improving interviewing skills—and the quality of hires.

Five Practical Purposes for an Interview

There are many reasons why interviews are conducted. Some companies view the interview strictly as a data collection session to determine if the candidate has the skills and abilities to be successful in the target position. Other companies see the interview as an opportunity to introduce the candidate to the culture by including facility tours and scheduling open discussions with people at different levels.

There are at least five purposes for almost any interview. The emphasis that you place on any one purpose can help you determine the structure of your next interview.

1. **Evaluate the candidate's ability to perform the job.** This is the big one. The interview should allow you to collect information that will help you accurately evaluate the candidate's skills and abilities compared with those required for current and future job success.
2. **Evaluate the candidate's fit to the job.** The most highly skilled candidates are not necessarily those who will thrive in your work environment. The interview helps you evaluate how the candidate's likes and dislikes mesh with the content of the job, the organization culture, the physical work environment, and the people with whom the candidate will work. (See Chapter 8 for more on this topic.)
3. **Provide a realistic job preview.** The interview is a unique opportunity to provide a candid snapshot of work life in your company. It's also an opportunity for the candidate to ask questions about any and all aspects of the job. Open discussion will encourage applicants who fit the job to pursue employment and discourage those who don't. There's nothing worse than a new hire saying, "If only I'd known that, I wouldn't have accepted the job."
4. **Sell the job.** Competition is extreme for the best people. During the interview you can effectively share selling points that might attract a candidate. It's amazing how many companies neglect to discuss their great benefits, such as career opportunities, retirement plans, training opportunities, child-care options, health club memberships, tuition reimbursement, awards that the company has won, and flexible hours.

Don't Oversell

TRICKS OF THE TRADE

When you interview, don't oversell the company or the position. Studies show that what people respect most is honesty. Things are not perfect in any company, and candidates know it. Be frank about the pros and cons of working in your company. Let the candidate talk to employees and see a few warts. It's better to lose people in the interview than six months later, after you've invested time and money in training.

5. **Complete the profile.** Most candidates will have provided a résumé, completed an application, or both. The interview provides a perfect opportunity to follow up on areas of interest and fill in missing information. This is especially helpful for technical positions where expertise with specific types of technology is important. Candidates complete résumés and applications with varying levels of detail and accuracy. Often, what appears to be meaningful is much less significant when you hear "the rest of the story." On the other hand, what appears to be insignificant may turn out to be quite meaningful.

Why Traditional Interviews Don't Work

Before you conduct the perfect interview, you need to understand the common mistakes that interviewers make. These mistakes (and their profound consequences) are recognizable across industries, job titles, and organization levels. We can easily recall very successful companies hiring clerical personnel who couldn't type, customer service reps who hated talking on the phone, team managers who lacked leadership ability, and executives who were poor strategic thinkers. Why? Some of the following interviewing mistakes certainly played a role.

- **Lack of clear interview purpose.** It's moments before your interview and you begin to wonder, "Just what is my goal for the next 60 minutes? Am I here to sell this candidate on my company? Should I be focusing on technical skills? Should I be trying to provide a realistic job preview? Should I use this time to allow the candidate to ask questions? Gee, I wonder what the other interviewers are covering." These are great questions. Just don't wait until the interview begins to think about them.
- **Lack of clearly defined position competencies.** Many interviewers take their best shot at asking questions that will give them insight into whether a candidate has "what it takes" to be successful. The problem is, in many cases

"what it takes" has not been defined. For any position, you can translate "what it takes" into the position competencies required for successful job performance. As discussed in Chapter 1, these are the categories of related knowledge, skills, abilities, and motivations required for job success.

Know Your Competencies

When you consider that most positions have between 8 and 14 position competency areas, it's easy to see how important information can be missed, if the competencies are not clearly defined. A common example is the company that hires the well-organized, highly experienced, highly skilled project manager. Later it turns out, after he has alienated his entire team, that the company did not interview thoroughly around key position competencies such as leadership style, coaching ability, flexibility, tolerance for stress, and general interpersonal skills.

- **Lack of interview structure.** You know the frustration of getting completely lost out on the road? The best remedy is a map that provides clear direction. Conducting an interview without structure is much like driving to an unknown location without a map. Like many of us who won't ask for directions or use a map, many interviewers try to choose the right candidate without a structured process to help them collect the right information. However, the stakes are much higher. You're not just wasting time. You could make a costly hiring mistake. An effective interview structure comes from creating an interview guide, built on position competencies, that contains planned questions and a structured rating format.
- **Lack of preparation.** Do you ever wing interviews? You know, a quick glance at the résumé or application and you're off to the interviewing races. We've done it—and it's a colossal waste of time. Because of the frantic pace of work, most interviewers are not adequately prepared even when they have a structured interview process to follow.

They present a harried, less than professional image to the candidate and miss important information along the way. Spending a few minutes reviewing the requirements for the job, the candidate's résumé or application, and the interview questions is necessary for conducting a productive interview.

- **Poor follow-up questioning techniques.** Many interviewers ask follow-up questions that reveal their bias about what they believe is the "right" answer. Similar to courtroom questions that "lead the witness," poorly constructed follow-up questions can help the candidate give the "right" answer. Savvy candidates are able to tailor their responses to the bias of the interviewer.

- **Legal liability.** Many otherwise good interviews have been derailed through a seemingly innocent comment. An employment attorney told us about a call he received from a manager who figured he was in trouble because he didn't use the right phrasing when asking a candidate about her disability. Although his intentions were good, his wording was inappropriate and his company had to take immediate action. Many of the topics you might normally discuss in conversation are taboo in a formal interview. It's critical to know the difference. As a general rule, anything that is not job-related is not appropriate.

- **Allowing bias to influence the interview.** In a typical interview, a candidate's fate is determined in the first two to five minutes. The interviewer's personal preferences, beliefs, likes, and dislikes—things that have nothing to do with the job—exert a powerful influence.

Avoiding Interview Bias

Companies spend billions of dollars each year betting on the fact that people do not make rational decisions. Just look at TV commercials. What does free falling out of an airplane attached to a snowboard have to do with the taste of Pepsi? A lot, obviously, because Pepsi and every other large soft drink

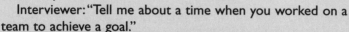

Tailoring Responses

Here's an interview that shows how a candidate can tailor responses to the interviewer's bias.

Interviewer: "Tell me about a time when you worked on a team to achieve a goal."

Candidate: "The task force was under a lot of pressure to complete the safety program. There were a couple of people on the team who were just plain difficult to get along with. In fact, there were a few blowups that I got stuck in the middle of. But overall we did a great job. Honestly, if someone doesn't want to be part of the team, I say we're better off without them."

So far, so good. But the follow-up questions may or may not elicit significant information about the candidate. Consider how questions can be ineffective when they reveal the interviewer's bias.

Interviewer: "OK, so are you saying that you don't always get along with people?"

Candidate: "Oh, no. I'm a people person. I get along with everyone."

(Few people would answer "yes" to such a blatantly negative question. A better follow-up would have been "Tell me about one of those blowups. What happened? How did it turn out?")

Interviewer: "Why do you feel that way about excluding people from teams? At our company, we try to help everyone to be an effective part of the team."

Candidate: "What I meant to convey is how important I think teamwork is and that everyone works together. We all win when the team wins, you know."

(No matter what the candidate really thinks, she now knows what answer to give. It would have been better for the interviewer to say, "Teams aren't for everyone. Tell me about the situation that led you to want to exclude one of the team members.")

company spend millions on these super action commercials each year. The fact is, whether we're making a decision to buy a beverage, choose a restaurant, or hire a new employee, we're easily influenced by our biases.

Bias: No One's Exempt

We can recall the staffing manager in a top firm wanting to hire a sales and marketing associate because she reminded him of his daughter. The fact that she scored low in the sales presentation, had average writing skills, and didn't particularly like prospecting was beside the point. Think about it—this manager teaches others how to interview! Bias is clearly one of the toughest challenges in the interview. Remember: NO ONE is exempt from bias!

"Interview bias might be an issue for some people but not me," you may be thinking. "I know what to look for and I'm fair." Maybe, but we doubt it. Every interviewer is influenced to some degree by personal preferences and past experiences that are unrelated to choosing the right candidate. The goal is to control bias by being aware of it and by using a structured interview that focuses on *behavior*. Let's look at the most common interview biases and what you can do to keep them in check.

Interview bias Any time an interviewer's evaluation of a candidate is influenced by anything that is not job-related.

Similarity bias Allowing a candidate's similarity or dissimilarity to you to influence your evaluation of his or her skills and abilities.

Similarity Bias

Have you ever noticed that if you talk to someone who shares certain characteristics with you, such as a similar background, beliefs or attitudes, hobbies, school, or hometown, you find it easier to like the person? We all feel more comfortable with people who are like us. The problem is that this familiarity often causes us to overlook important weaknesses in a person. This is called *similarity bias*.

The opposite of similarity bias occurs when someone appears, at least on the surface, to be very different from us. We tend to overlook the positive and emphasize the negative in people who look different, talk differently, or have different attitudes and beliefs.

First Impression Bias

Have you ever seen someone and instantly known that you didn't like him or her? We tend to form opinions about others very quickly. This is called *first impression bias.*

This is actually a very adaptive response that can help us avoid dangerous situations. Unfortunately, it's difficult for us to consciously turn it on and off. We usually form impressions quickly. Then we tend to look for

> **First impression bias**
> Making an overall judgment about an individual based on job-irrelevant data collected during the first few minutes of an interview.

Key Term

further information to confirm our initial impression and ignore information that might undermine it.

Halo Error

Have you ever assumed that just because a candidate has great technical skills, he or she will make a good leader? We often let one characteristic of a person influence our perception of the entire person. This is referred to as *halo error* because we tend to place a halo above people who rate highly in one or two competencies and just assume that

---

Do Looks Count?

For Example

The news magazine program *20/20* conducted an informal study to test first impression bias. The show sent two "candidates" (actors) to interview for the same job. One had great looks but an average résumé and a quiet personality. The other had average looks but a great résumé and a nice social style. In every instance, the more attractive candidate was chosen over the less attractive, more qualified one. When the interviewers were let in on the secret, most could not believe how easily they were influenced. In another study, first-graders chose an attractive, less interpersonal substitute teacher over a substitute who was less attractive, but very interactive. Such findings have been replicated many times in research, pointing to the need for us to focus on *behavior* rather than *impression.*

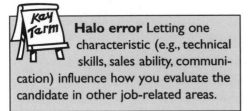

Halo error Letting one characteristic (e.g., technical skills, sales ability, communication) influence how you evaluate the candidate in other job-related areas.

they're good at everything else. It happens all the time. For instance, we tend to assume that top salespeople will make good sales managers and that skilled engineers will make competent team leaders.

Pressure-to-Fill-Positions Bias

Here's the scenario. You're the manager of recruitment and selection, you have five major projects going on, and your

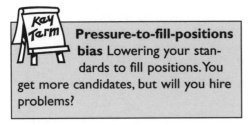

Pressure-to-fill-positions bias Lowering your standards to fill positions. You get more candidates, but will you hire problems?

internal clients are demanding that you fill positions that needed to be filled yesterday! The next thing you know, you're doing an interview and, although the candidate is not really acceptable, you pass him or her on. This is known as *pressure-to-fill-positions bias*.

This scenario understandably happens all the time—especially now, when there is more demand for skills and abilities that are harder to find. But even when the troops are breathing down your neck, it's better to wait for the high performer than to be stuck with a dud. You'll wish you'd stuck to the original criteria when it comes time to justify the costs of recruiting, interviewing, training, and lost productivity associated with the poor performer.

Contrast Effects

You've just finished interviewing five terrible candidates. The next person who comes in the door is, in reality, a below-average candidate, one you would normally not hire. However, after the five terrible candidates, this person looks acceptable, so you make a job offer. You've just made a poor decision based on the *contrast effect bias.*

Contrast effect bias
When an evaluation of a candidate is influenced by your evaluations of other candidates.

Unless you use fixed standards for evaluation—evaluating candidates according to established criteria and not by comparing them with one another—you'll always have this problem. It is very possible that, on a given day, you could interview five acceptable candidates, and then interview twenty consecutive unacceptable candidates over the next three days.

Recognizing and Avoiding Bias

Table 6-1 summarizes the specific problems that result from biases and presents some ideas to help minimize the effects of bias on your hiring decisions.

Being aware of our natural tendencies toward bias is an important first step toward conducting interviews that are more effective and more job-related. However, curbing these tendencies can be difficult without the proper support. You can find such support in *competency-based, structured interviewing.* Let's take a look at how it can help you become a better interviewer.

Competency-Based Interviewing

Let's face it. If you don't focus the interview on the position competencies (knowledge, skills, abilities, and motivations) required for job success, how good can the results be? Sure, you might tap into some important skill areas, but you will definitely miss some. The areas you miss will make you scratch your head and ask, "What could I have done different-ly?" Generally, the answer is "a lot," beginning with a thorough analysis of the critical competencies required for success in the target position. (See Chapter 1 for a closer look at compe-tency analysis.) The results of the competency analysis will help you focus the interview on relevant topics (i.e., job-relat-ed competencies).

Bias	Issues and Problems	How to Control It
Similarity	• Weaknesses are overlooked in similar candidates and strengths are discounted in dissimilar candidates. • EEOC guidelines strictly prohibit the use of selection criteria that are not job-related.	• Ask yourself how similar or dissimilar you are to the candidate and how it is affecting your judgment. • Do not spend significant time discussing matters that are not job-related.
First Impression	• Initial candidate impression (hair, accent, clothing) creates bias that affects judgment in job-related areas. • Most interviewers are not aware how much they are affected by this type of bias.	• Be aware that impressions formed in the first two minutes of the interview significantly affect the outcome. • Try to pinpoint what you like and dislike about the candidate within the first five minutes of the interview. Make yourself aware of how you feel so that it won't color your judgment in job-relevant areas.
Halo Effect	• Most positions have between 8 and 14 separate competency areas. Ability in one area is generally a poor predictor of success in all competencies.	• Evaluate each position competency separately. Be careful not to let the ratings from one competency influence ratings in other competencies.
Pressure to Fill Positions	• Lowering standards to fill positions results in tremendous cost to your company. • EEOC guidelines require that all job candidates be treated fairly and that the hiring requirements are the same for everyone.	• Create an awareness among hiring managers about the cost of poor selection. • Initiate an ongoing staffing strategy to ensure that quality candidates are always in the pipeline.

Table 6-1. Issues and problems with bias and how to deal with them

Bias	Issues and Problems	How to Control It
Contrast Effects	• Comparing candidates can cause you to lower or raise your expectations from one candidate to the next. Usually results in an otherwise unacceptable candidate being hired.	• Establish performance standards for each competency area that you are evaluating. • Make a concerted effort to compare each candidate to the standards for the position and not to other candidates.

Table 6-1, continued

Let's take a look at the four steps for developing a competency-based interview.

1. Conduct a thorough competency analysis. The basic steps include:
   • Review the current job description for the target position.
   • Interview current employees about what they do on the job.
   • If necessary, observe someone performing the job.
   • Consider how the job will change in the future.
   • Consider characteristics of the job that will impact job fit (e.g., work culture, work environment, travel schedule, company values).
2. Categorize related knowledge, skills, abilities, and motivations from step 1 into position competencies. In general, most positions require at least 8, but no more than 14 position competencies. (See Chapter 1 for more specific guidelines.)
3. Decide which competencies you want to cover in the interview. You may not be able to adequately cover every position competency in the interview, especially if you have 30 minutes for an interview and ten competencies to cover.
   • Interview around the competencies that are most important to successful job performance and that are least covered elsewhere in your selection system.

- If you have more than one interview step in your selection process (i.e., screening interview and final interview) or multiple final interviewers for each candidate, you may be able to cover all of the position competencies. There should be some overlap on the most critical competencies, and each competency should be covered in at least one interview.

4. Develop a structured interview process that effectively assesses the competencies identified in step 3.

This last step is critical. It is entirely possible to do a really good job with steps 1 through 3 and still end up with a lousy interview process. Let's take a look at what you need to do to prevent this.

Structured Interviewing

Over the last 20 years, interviews have evolved from general discussions requiring little planning to structured interviews complete with interview guides, predetermined questions, structured rating formats, and special interview training.

Why the big shift to structured interviewing? The answer is simple. Structured interviews have been found, time and time again, to be the most practical and effective type of interview. You can collect more accurate information, in more job-related areas, in the least amount of time. In addition, because of the structure, almost anyone can be trained to conduct consistent, productive interviews.

> **Key Term**
>
> **Structured Interview**
> A planned discussion, usually between a job candidate and a company representative, with the following components:
> *Interview Guide*—A guide to facilitate the interview.
> *Predetermined Questions*—Planned questions to elicit information in position competency areas.
> *Structured Rating Format*—A standard rating system to evaluate the information collected during the interview.
> *Training*—Some form of guidance (written, video, classroom) on how to use the process.

For years, interviewing has been, more or less, considered an art. Results varied dramatically by interviewer. Structure has made interviewing more of a science—allowing us to study every part of the interview, find out what works, develop components, try out new methods, and provide detailed directions for using the process. As such, the results can be remarkably reliable, across time and across interviewers.

Conversely, unstructured interviews have been found to be the most unreliable and inaccurate interviewing approach, with results equal to those of a blind guess. No matter how well you interview, unstructured interviews produce unreliable data.

The goal is accurate candidate information. There are a variety of structured interviewing formats that will achieve this goal. And believe it or not, none of them involve palm reading, handwriting analysis, or asking the candidate to explain what kind of animal he or she would be if given the choice. The most popular and easy to learn structured interviewing formats are Past Behavior Interview Questions, Structured Role-Plays, and Structured Situational Questions. The next chapter provides a closer look at each of these structured interviewing techniques and tells you more about how to conduct a structured interview.

Manager's Checklist for Chapter 6

❑ Interviewing is one of the most widely used hiring techniques, but it's often misapplied, with the result that poor candidates are offered jobs while qualified candidates are missed.

❑ There are five purposes for interviewing: (1) evaluate a candidate's ability to do the job, (2) evaluate the candidate's job fit, (3) provide the candidate with a realistic job preview, (4) sell the job, and (5) get a complete profile of the candidate to supplement résumés, applications, and other documentation.

❏ Interviewers often fail because they don't establish a good purpose for the interview, have not properly prepared for the interview, and don't have a good way of structuring the interview or of asking questions that will elicit useful responses.

❏ There is much potential for interviewer bias, and it's important to be aware of this and minimize its effect on hiring decisions.

❏ One good interviewing method is the competency-based approach. To do this, you determine which competencies the job calls for and then use the interview to learn more about the candidate's fit to these competencies.

❏ A structured interview is a formal interviewing process that allows the interviewer to learn more about candidates and determine which ones would fit best and perform at the highest levels.

Structured Interviewing Techniques

John tried not to appear nervous as he waited for the interview to begin. He was sitting in a chair at the head of the table, facing a panel of interviewers from Big One Bank. Having passed a one-on-one screening interview, John was invited back for an in-depth interview with the bank management team. He was told that this was going to be a standard interview. All entry-level managerial applicants must meet with panel approval in order to be hired.

Introductions were made, and John was told that each member of the panel would take turns asking him questions. The atmosphere was relaxed, and John began to feel at ease. The interviewers debated for a moment, deciding which one would begin the questioning. Then it started.

"In three words or less, what's your definition of a good leader?" asked one of the suit-clad managers.

"In my opinion, a good leader is a good motivator, a good communicator, and a wise delegator," John confidently responded after pausing for thought. "Whew," John thought. "They started off with an easy one—just to break the ice."

And, judging from the nodding and murmuring going around the table, he must have nailed the answer. "I bet they liked how I used words that ended in *or*."

"Who's your favorite cartoon character and why?" asked the next manager. John thought he was joking. However, the other managers smiled and nodded approvingly.

"That's a good one. When did you come up with that question?" asked another manager.

"Over lunch, when I was thinking up questions to ask," responded the manager who originated the question. "I'll have to write it down, so I can use it from now on," he added.

John was speechless. But, they were all looking at him, expecting an answer. "Well, uh, I guess I would have to say Richie Rich is my favorite cartoon character, because, uh, he appears to make good investments and manage money very well," John tentatively offered—trying as best he could to think of a job-relevant response to the idiotic question.

Again with smiles and nods, the managers looked pleased with his response. John was less than pleased. He thought, "This was supposed to be a standard interview. What are they doing here? What am I doing here?"

What happened?

Big One Bank thought it had a standard interview process for hiring managers—every applicant was subjected to the same steps. Unfortunately, the content of those standardized steps was not structured with any job-relevant criteria in mind. Hiring managers were left to come up with questions to ask job candidates. As a result, the hiring review panel ended up asking different questions of different applicants—many of them theoretical and irrelevant to the job. And, you can bet that the method used to evaluate candidate responses was just as subjective. A truly structured approach to interviewing involves standardizing not only the interviewing process but also the interview content and the method of evaluation.

In this chapter you will learn effective interviewing techniques that relate to the following topics:

- Past behavior interview questions
- Structured role-plays
- Structured situational questions
- Conducting the interview

Past Behavior Interview Questions

If you're going to use just one questioning format, this is it. The past behavior interview is the most popular, versatile, and easy to use structured format. The concept here is that past behavior is the best predictor of future behavior.

When a friend of mine was 18 years old, his mother said, "When you choose the girl who will be your wife, you better love her just the way she is; she's not going to change, and neither are you." It's true. People, for the most part, don't change their behavior from year to year. For example, if you've always been meticulous about keeping your car clean in the past, there's a good chance you'll have a clean car tomorrow. If you're notorious for showing up late, no one is shocked when you're late for the next meeting. Whether we're talking about interpersonal style, safety on the job, problem-solving ability, or any other behavior, find out what a person's pattern of behavior has been in the past and you will have a good indicator of his or her behavior in the future.

So how do you structure questions that will give you an accurate picture of past behavior? The first step is to under-stand what a behavioral response looks like in an interview.

Identifying Behavioral Responses

As an interviewer, you need to be able to distinguish between behavioral and nonbehavioral responses. It's very common for articulate candidates to theorize or give impressive opinions about why they would make stellar performers. When you ask those same candidates to provide past examples of the stellar performance, the answers are often less impressive. For example, a candidate says, "I always head big projects with large budgets." What does this tell you about what this person has actually done? Nothing. You don't really know what this answer means until the candidate gives you a specific example of one project, a detailed accounting of his or her responsibilities, and an explanation of the project results.

Specific examples of what a candidate has done are much more important than what the candidate tells you he or she *usually* does, *always* does, *can* do, *would* do, *could* do, or *should* do. Remember: saying it and doing it are two very different things.

Behavioral Response A response that describes what the candidate has actually said or done in a specific situation. A behavioral response should contain the background of the situation, the action that the candidate took, and the result of the action.

Nonbehavioral Response A response that is theoretical or vague or an opinion.

Candidates give theoretical, nonbehavioral responses so often that we don't even realize we're listening to an opinion about what they might do, instead of an example of what they did. It's usually easy enough to know the right things to say or do in a hypothetical situation. But when we're caught up in reality, facing all those little details that can make managing such a challenge, it's far less easy to say and do the right things. You should judge candidates by what they've said and done in reality, not what they would say and do in theory. Candidates give theoretical answers every day—and many end up getting the job.

Would, Could, Should Any time a candidate's answer includes theoretical terms (would, could, or should) or vague terms (always, usually, sometimes, all the time, often) you may be collecting a nonbehavioral response. When you hear these words, be sure to ask for the background of a specific situation, the action taken, and the result.

Think of the interviewer who asks the truly inept project manager candidate how he or she manages projects. The impressive textbook answer comes back in a long oration about Gantt charts,

PERT charts, and the importance of disciplined and prioritized delegation. Another theoretical answer. The interviewer accepts the answer at face value, doesn't ask for behavioral examples, and makes a big mistake by hiring the inept candidate.

Let's be clear. Just because someone knows the right answer doesn't mean he or she can apply it on the job. In fact, very often they can't, they haven't, and they won't. The best way to know if candidates can really do the things they are talking about is to collect past behavioral examples. The problem is, the less articulate candidate who could provide really meaningful past behavioral examples is often outshone by the more articulate nonperformer who speaks in vague and theoretical terms. This is why it's so important for interviewers to get in the practice of asking for and recognizing specific examples of past behavior.

Asking Behavioral Questions

You've just begun the interview. You ask the customer service supervisor candidate to give you an example of the most difficult customer problem he's had to solve in the last two months. He replies with a theoretical answer, explaining his opinion about solving problems on the job.

You immediately realize that he did not give you a past behavioral example. So, you follow up your initial question by saying something like, "I see, but what I really need is an actual example of a customer problem that you encountered, the actions that you took to solve it, and the results of those actions." This time, the candidate responds by telling you a detailed story about an actual customer complaint and how he dealt with it.

You did it! Now you're learning about the candidate's past behavior.

Essentially, you get what you ask for in an interview. Therefore, your interview questions and follow-up questions should ask for behavioral examples. The following introduc-

Evaluating Initiative

Let's take a look at the difference between a behavioral and a nonbehavioral response. To evaluate the competency "initiative," an interviewer tells each candidate, "Describe a time when you did more than what was expected on the job." Look at the replies from two different candidates. Remember: a behavioral response includes the situation, the action, and the result of that action.

Behavioral Answer: "I remember one time when I was new in the information systems department, and even though I wasn't a programmer (background), I decided on my own to take a course on programming so that I would know what my boss meant when she needed something done (action). My boss was so pleased that she asked some of her other reports to take similar courses (result)."

This response gives a background, an action, and the result. This is what you want.

Nonbehavioral Answer: "I take initiative on the job all the time. In my department, everybody pitches in and does whatever it takes to get the job done. I really believe that employees should realize that everyone has to wear a lot of different hats. If I were in a situation where it would help the team for me to learn additional tasks or take on more responsibility, I definitely would do it without being asked."

This is a great example of what you don't want. There are six red flags in this response! Yet many interviewers would be tricked by how good this response sounds. The candidate seems enthusiastic and willing to take initiative to help the team. That's great! But what has she actually done?

tions to behavioral questions help solicit behavioral responses. Use them often.

"Give me an example of a time when …"

"Tell me about a specific situation where you …"

"Have you ever been in [such and such] a situation? Tell me about one of those times."

On the other hand, the introductions below will likely get you opinions or hypothetical responses. If you ask these, you

will surely need to follow up with one of the behavioral questions above. So don't waste your time with them.

"How do you feel about ..."

"What would you do if ..."

"How might you have ..."

Finally, avoid questions that are leading. Leading questions will usually get a simple "yes" or "no" response.

"Do you get a lot of satisfaction out of making a big sale?"

"You don't mind working overtime, do you?"

"Did your idea work?"

Table 7-1 shows the differences between theoretical questions, leading questions, and planned behavioral questions. As
you read the questions, think about how candidates would
likely respond to them. Notice that you can attempt to assess
the same competencies using the three types of questions—
and get very different responses.

Use a Consistent Rating Process

In the smash hit musical *Miss Saigon*, there's a scene where a
full-sized helicopter descends onto the stage. As the play
ended, a friend's wife had tears in her eyes, moved by the
passionate love story. She looked at my friend and in a soft
voice said, "You're thinking about how they got that damned
helicopter on stage, aren't you?" Sadly enough, he told us, he
was. They perceived the scene quite differently.

The same thing happens with the information we gather in
interviews. Although interviewers are processing the same
candidate information, their standards for acceptable behavior
may differ considerably. Without standardized rating scales,
the result is generally very different interpretations.

The most widely used standardized rating scales are
numerical. Structured interviews commonly use between three
and ten points. Some include behavioral descriptions for each
point on the rating scale.

If you're developing your own standardized rating scale, a
five-point scale, with or without behavioral descriptions, is

Com-petency	Theoretical Question	Leading Question	Behavioral Question
Teamwork	How would you handle difficult employees?	Are you good at handling conflict?	As a supervisor, tell me about a time when you had to coach a difficult employee.
Sales Ability	Why do you think you can sell?	We have pretty demanding sales goals here. Are you up to the challenge?	Describe the largest sale you've made in the last 12 months. How did you do it?
Problem Solving	How do you go about solving manufacturing problems that arise?	Can you trouble-shoot equipment problems?	Tell me about a recent problem (equipment, processes, quality) that you faced in your job. What did you do to resolve it?
Safety Orientation	How important do you feel safety is on the job?	It sounds like you're a safe worker. Right?	Tell me about conditions that you've encountered that you consider unsafe. What were the conditions? What did you do?
Adaptability	How would you feel if you had to adjust your schedule to changing demands?	So, when you were moved into the four different positions in one month, it didn't bother you?	Tell me about a time when you had to adjust to changes on the job. What happened? How did it turn out?

Table 7-1. Differences between theoretical, leading, and behavioral questions

very effective. Research indicates that behavioral descriptions do not make the rating scale more valid. However, they help train new interviewers and provide a sense of common understanding among multiple interviewers.

Rating Scale with Behavioral Descriptions				
1	2	3	4	5
Showed little ability to adapt to change; viewed trivial changes as major obstacles.	Attempted to adapt to change; did not favor the change; sensitive to minor changes; work performance suffered.	Accepted change; learned new information in a timely manner; work performance did not suffer.	Enjoyed change; adapted quickly to new task or environment; work performance improved.	Clearly enjoyed change; adapted quickly; performance improved; demonstrated a history of successful adaptation.
Rating Scale without Behavioral Descriptions				
Much less than acceptable	Less than acceptable	Acceptable	More than acceptable	Much more than acceptable

Table 7-2. Standardized rating scales for the competency "adaptability"

Each competency area is evaluated separately, using a separate standardized rating scale. Table 7-2 shows two five-point standardized rating scales for the competency "adaptability"—one with behavioral descriptions and one without.

Although the past behavior interviewing technique is the most commonly used structured interviewing method, there are two other techniques that can provide information that may be missed by the past behavior interview questions. They are structured role-plays and structured situational questions.

Structured Role-Plays

We have been browbeaten and fired by numerous candidates during interviews. Hard to believe? Not if you consider that the candidates were role-playing leaders conducting performance discussions with me, an employee with an attitude.

It's amazing how a candidate's true colors come out during a role-play. Many companies use role-plays in their

> **Structured interview role-play** A planned interaction during which the candidate and the interviewer act out a hypothetical workplace scenario.

Guidelines for Interview Role-plays

Role-plays are effective for evaluating interpersonal competencies such as teamwork, coaching, customer service, and leadership style.

Role-plays should be based on actual situations that the candidate would face on the job.

There's no evidence to suggest that long role-plays (30 to 60 minutes) are more valid than multiple, short role-plays (5 to 10 minutes).

Give the candidate instructions that clearly explain the role he or she will play. For example, the instructions may assign the role of a customer service representative who will be talking on the phone to a dissatisfied customer. The instructions should also provide background information so the candidate can understand the situation and prepare for the interaction.

The interviewer should have clear guidelines explaining how to role-play with the candidate.

The interviewer should receive training and have the opportunity to practice the role-play prior to the interview.

A standardized rating scale should be used to evaluate the candidate's behavior.

interviewing process. Call centers use telephone role-plays to evaluate customer service skills. Manufacturing companies use peer role-plays to evaluate how candidates will interact in a team environment and supervisor role-plays to evaluate the coaching style of leadership candidates.

Structured interview questions The interviewer presents a brief description of a situation that would likely occur on the job and asks the candidate how he or she would behave in that situation.

Structured Situational Questions

Over the last ten years we've spent many hours training interviewers not to ask candidates what they would do, but to focus on things they have actually done. In fact, that's what you read just a few pages back. However, situational questions are an important exception to the "past behavior only" rule.

Here are some of the advantages of including situational questions in your interview:

- Candidates without a lot of experience (past behavior) can demonstrate their potential.
- You can present all candidates with in-depth situations in a structured, consistent format.
- You can explore a variety of unique, job-specific situations in a short period of time.
- Situational questions are easy to use. The interviewer or the candidate simply reads the situational question and the candidate responds.

Let's look at a structured situational interview question used by a telecommunications company for evaluating problem solving among candidates for customer service representative positions. With a situational interview question, the interviewer would ask the candidate to read a written description of a scenario, like the one below:

> You are the coordinator of the customer service department for a cellular phone company. There are several positions within the customer service department, including General Information Representatives, Plan Choice Specialists, Billing Specialists, and Retention Specialists. All representatives take incoming calls from the same toll-free line.
>
> Current and potential customers who call the toll-free line are connected with the first available representative. Once the customer explains the nature of the call, the representative transfers him or her to the appropriate representative.
>
> The customer service representatives have mentioned that customers have been complaining about being transferred to different representatives and being placed on hold for long periods of time. The Retention Specialists, who are paid mainly on commission, are particularly upset, because dealing with a frustrated customer, who already plans to discontinue service, makes their job even harder. Think about what you would do in this situation.

The interviewer would then ask the candidates the following questions:

- What problems do you see?
- What additional information do you want to know? How would you gather it?
- What do you perceive as your options?
- Which option would you choose? Why?
- What do you think would happen? Why?
- How would you know if your solutions worked?

The interviewer would review the candidate's responses to these questions and rate the candidate's level of problem solving using a structured rating scale similar to the ones shown earlier, in the section on past behavior interviewing.

As with past behavioral questions, situational questions should never be followed up with leading questions. Think about it. You're asking the candidate to hypothesize about what he or she would do in the situation, with complete freedom to take the situation in any direction. Why would you want to lead the candidate with your questions?

Conducting the Interview

A friend of ours will never forget one of her first interviews after finishing school. She walked into the human resources manager's office. Without looking up, he gestured for her to take a seat on what amounted to a kid's Barney chair located directly in front of his gargantuan desk. Without so much as a hello, he started grilling her about her work experience (of which she had very little). By the end of the interview, she was sure that no amount of money could convince her to participate in a second interview.

This experience taught her that there's much more to an effective interview than a structured set of questions. Let's look at what else you need to consider when conducting an interview. **Review the candidate's background information.** It takes only a few minutes for a candidate to realize that you haven't taken the time to familiarize yourself with his or her résumé or appli-

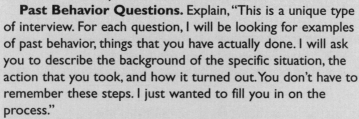

A Successful Beginning

If you address the following points in the introduction to the interview, you will help candidates understand the objectives:

Past Behavior Questions. Explain, "This is a unique type of interview. For each question, I will be looking for examples of past behavior, things that you have actually done. I will ask you to describe the background of the specific situation, the action that you took, and how it turned out. You don't have to remember these steps. I just wanted to fill you in on the process."

Note Taking. Explain, "I'll be taking notes during the interview so I don't forget anything you tell me. So if you see me looking down, I'm not disinterested. I just want to make sure I capture what you're saying." Taking notes is especially important if you're interviewing multiple candidates and discussing the results with other interviewers.

Pacing. Explain, "There are a lot of areas to cover during the interview. To make sure that you have a fair chance to answer all the questions, I may stop you during an answer and move on to the next question." Don't hesitate to pace the interview, even if it means interrupting a talkative candidate numerous times. Getting through the entire interview is truly in the best interest of the candidate and your company.

cation. You'll impress the candidate and ask better questions if you take time just before the interview to review the candidate's background information, highlight areas where you want to follow up, and pronounce his or her name correctly.

Choose the right setting. It's never a good idea for a candidate to be uncomfortable or intimidated during an interview. A relaxed environment is more conducive to creating a positive company image and eliciting accurate information, both positive and negative. If possible, conduct the interview sitting at a table or around the corner of a desk. Also, be on time. Showing up late for an interview conveys a message that the candidate's time is not valuable.

Make the candidate feel welcome. Smile and take a minute to say hello. Let the candidate know how you appreciate the interview. Being friendly will not lessen your impact or reduce your negotiating position. On the contrary, the candidate will open up and want the job even more.

Choose a dress style that matches the position and work environment. For example, if you are interviewing a candidate for a manufacturing position, don't wear a suit.

Explain the interview format. Candidates who are used to traditional, unstructured interviews may feel confused by the format of a structured interview. Explaining the purpose and sequence of the interview will help candidates concentrate by addressing questions that they'll likely have (but probably not ask).

Listen to the candidate. The candidate should do 80% of the talking. Listen closely to what he or she is saying. Many times when candidates are answering questions about one competency area, they provide valuable input about a completely different area. You need to be tuned in and take note so that you can follow up.

Ask for details. Get specific. For example, if a candidate says, "I was responsible for the project," ask, "Exactly what were your responsibilities? Give me examples of how you carried them out. What were the results of the projects?" Do not settle for general statements. Ask follow-up questions that elicit specific examples of past behavior. Observe the candidate's body language. Facial expressions can reveal a lot about feelings. You can observe signs of enthusiasm, boredom, disagreement, disinterest, and attentiveness. How people sit, their eye contact, and the tone and volume of their voice provide an indication of their confidence and belief in what they are saying.

Maintain the candidate's self-esteem. Interviews can be very stressful, especially for candidates who are reentering the workforce after raising children or being laid off, candidates with very little work experience, or candidates who speak English as a second language. Make sure that these candi-

Maintaining Self-Esteem

Here are a few ways to help maintain a candidate's self-esteem:

Smile. It's OK to smile or even laugh at a humorous story.

Empathize. In response to a particularly trying situation, you could simply say, "That must have been difficult." Be careful not to convey the message that you agree or disagree with the action the candidate took.

Rationalization. Before asking a candidate for a negative example of work performance, provide a rationalization statement. This gives the candidate permission to talk about less than satisfactory performance. For example, if asking for a negative example of decision making, you could begin by stating, "We all make decisions that we live to regret." Then ask the question, "Tell me about a decision you would like to take back. What was the situation? What decision did you make? How did it turn out?"

Know When to Move On. Candidates will sometimes discuss past events that are painful for them to recall, such as a divorce, death in the family, getting fired from a job, or an arrest. It's inappropriate to discuss any situation (especially painful memories) that is not job-related. If the experience is job-related, you should collect the basic facts and move on. If you probe too much, you risk embarrassing the candidate and having him or her shut down during the rest of the discussion.

dates feel comfortable and secure enough to open up during the interview. Candidates who feel intimidated have the tendency to calculate their answers and withhold examples of negative past behaviors.

Allow plenty of time. You can't rush through a structured interview and collect good information. In an effective interview, the candidate responds to each question with a short story about past experience. You need to allow time for the candidate to recall specific experiences and explain them. As a guideline, you should allow ten minutes to open the interview, ten minutes to close the interview, and five to ten minutes for each competency area.

Evaluating Your Interview Process

Once you have your interviewing process in place and begin to use it, sit back and take a good hard look at it.

First, review your interview questions. Are they eliciting good responses? You may find that candidates cannot relate to a question, because of the way it's worded. If you consistently get a dumbfounded look in response to a question, you may need to tweak it.

Next, review your rating scales. Are they helpful? Or are you having a tough time assigning ratings for certain competencies? Check with any other interviewers to see if they're having similar problems. If so, you may need to more clearly define your scales.

Finally, look at the quality of hires. This is the big one. Are the people who are passing the interview performing well on the job? To answer this question, you can simply ask their supervisors how they feel about the quality of the new hires. You can do this right away. Later on, after the employee has been on the job for at least several months, you can formally assess how well the interview predicted job performance by doing a validation study. In Chapter 9, you'll learn more about how to do this.

Manager's Checklist for Chapter 7

❏ Determine in advance which interviewing techniques you would like to use.

❏ Develop structured questions for each competency area that you want to assess during the interview. Make sure your questions are job-relevant and behavioral.

❏ Prepare a comfortable setting and review all applicant materials ahead of time.

❏ Explain the structured interview process to the candidate so he or she can relax and concentrate on the questions.

❑ Incorporate the past behavior interviewing technique into your interview structure, because past behavior is a good indicator of future behavior.

❑ Ask candidates to provide specific examples of situations in which they were involved, including background, action taken, and results.

❑ Evaluate behavioral responses with a multipoint rating system.

❑ Use role-play and situational questions tools to gauge a candidate's response to hypothetical job situations.

❑ Use a structured rating system to evaluate each candidate on each position competency.

❑ Pace the interview to ensure that all competency areas are covered.

❑ Be aware of your biases.

❑ Help maintain the candidate's self-esteem.

❑ Review the interview process to determine if candidates are giving useful responses to your questions, if your rating system has proven helpful, and if the process has resulted in successful hires.

Evaluating Motivation to Perform the Job

You're the HR manager for a large call center. Most positions in the center are telephone customer service representatives. The job requires representatives to take calls from customers who have questions about products they've purchased from your firm. Typically, a representative will spend 90% of the eight-hour work day on the phone talking with between 70 and 90 customers. Some of these customers will have simple questions, and others will be upset about their product.

Usually, the people that you hire can do the job. Your selection process is quite complete and effectively screens out candidates who can't perform the job well. The process includes a face-to-face interview, a personality test, and a cognitive ability test. New hires go through a three-week training program, and it usually takes another three weeks to prepare them to handle the broad range of customer needs.

The problem is turnover. More than 60% of your hires leave within the first two months on the job. The remaining 40% tend to stay for one to three years. The high turnover within the first two months costs the company a lot in terms of service quality and the time and money invested in hiring and training. You've done some exit interviews and found that 60% were leaving because they didn't like the job, 20% because of the pay, and the remaining 20% for miscellaneous reasons.

What happened?

One thing that doesn't appear to have entered into the selection process is "motivational fit," the candidate's interest in doing the job. Motivational fit is a key component in determining whether a person will remain on the job, even more so than whether or not he or she can perform the job.

This chapter provides an overview of motivational fit, why it's important, and some methods for evaluating it. Specifically, the chapter covers the following topics:

- What is motivational fit?
- A holistic perspective of work
- Interview approaches for evaluating motivational fit
- Other means of evaluating motivational fit
- But no one really wants to do this job!
- What about college students and part-time employees?

What Is Motivational Fit?

There are probably a lot of jobs that most people could perform quite well. Just as an example, let's say that you are qualified (in terms of skills and abilities) to perform a hundred jobs. Of those hundred jobs, you would definitely not be interested in fifty of them. You would be willing to perform twenty of them, like to perform twenty of them, and love to perform ten of them. We would consider your motivational fit to be highest for the jobs you love and lowest for the ones you would definitely not be interested in doing.

If we could get you into one of the jobs you love, you'd probably do very well and stay for a long time. You would be more likely to work for less pay, put in more time, and commute farther for those jobs. By contrast, if you were to take one of the jobs that you were merely willing to do, you would be much less likely to stay very long, unless the job offered something important to you (like a higher salary or great colleagues) that you could not find elsewhere.

> **Key Term**
>
> **Motivational fit** The level of alignment or agreement between what a person expects or wishes to receive from a job and what the job can actually offer. These factors can include aspects of the work itself (such as using a certain type of software) or characteristics associated with the work (such as the pay, the schedule, or the style of supervision).

Motivational fit tends to relate more to what psychologists call "withdrawal behaviors" than actual job performance. Withdrawal behaviors include tardiness, absenteeism, use of sick days, and turnover. In other words, people who have a poor "fit" with their job may do their job well—they just look for ways to avoid doing it!

A Holistic Perspective of Work

Before we talk about how you can try to evaluate a person's motivational fit for a particular position, it's helpful to consider work from a broader perspective than we normally do. Table 8-1 covers a wide range of factors that differ from job to job and company to company. The table is broken into *intrinsic* and *extrinsic* job factors.

> **Key Term**
>
> **Intrinsic job factors** Aspects of work activities, what a person actually does on the job. For instance, intrinsic factors for a salesperson involve working with customers and the challenge of presenting a product or service, of negotiating with a customer over price or delivery schedule, and of competing with others.
>
> **Extrinsic job factors** Aspects related to the job, other than the work itself. For a salesperson, extrinsic factors would include the level and style of compensation, the amount of travel required, and the work schedule.

Research consistently shows that intrinsic factors are more important determinants of job satisfaction and withdrawal behaviors than are extrinsic factors. In other

Intrinsic Factors	Aspects that Differ from Job to Job
Variety	How routine is the job?
Autonomy	How much freedom do you have on the job?
Feedback from the Job	Do you know if you're doing a good job without someone telling you?
Part vs. Whole	Do you make a complete thing or just part of something?
Interaction with Co-workers	How much interaction do you have with others?
Work Environment	Do you work in an office, in a plant, in a warehouse, or outside?
Extrinsic Factors	
Style of Compensation	How are you paid? Hourly and overtime, salary and commission?
Level of Compensation	How well are you paid compared with other people with similar skills?
Opportunity for Promotion	Do you have a chance to move up? How fast? How far?
Supervisory Style	What is your supervisor like? Traditional or more empowering?
Work Schedule	When do you work? Night shift, 9 to 5, flexible, alternating shifts?
Commuting Distance	How long does it take you to get to work?
Benefits	What type of retirement and health benefits does the company offer?
Job Stability	How confident are you that this job will be here next year?
Day Care	Does the company offer some type of day care service?

Table 8-1. Factors that differentiate one job from another

words, people who enjoy what they are doing (high intrinsic rewards) report higher levels of job satisfaction and exhibit fewer withdrawal behaviors. However, people who are happy with their extrinsic rewards (e.g., pay) do not necessarily report higher levels of job satisfaction. In fact, if you are happy with the extrinsic rewards, yet hate the work (i.e., the job offers few intrinsic rewards), you will likely report low levels of job satisfaction. People can become trapped in positions they don't like because they can't find another job that provides as many extrinsic benefits. Often, people in these situations feel the need to "escape" from the actual work itself and will more likely engage in the withdrawal behaviors mentioned earlier.

Obviously there are other factors that influence whether or not a person will be happy in a job. The list in Table 8-1 is by no means exhaustive. However, it should serve as a solid base for considering what factors affect job fit and for determining whether a candidate will likely fit well into the job.

Interview Approaches for Evaluating Motivational Fit

It could be argued that most interviews are really "job fit" interviews. The interviewer is trying to determine whether or not the candidate will fit well in the job. One problem, however, is that interviewers look only at a candidate's skills and abilities to determine if he or she will "fit" the job. They never explore motivation to do the job. This is problematic because a person can have all the skills, education, and knowledge to perform the job effectively, yet still be a poor fit for the job.

In order to get a more complete picture of how well the person fits the job, you need to directly assess the applicant's interests and motivations, as well as his or her skills and abilities. One of the most highly effective methods for assessing motivational fit is also the most straightforward method—simply ask the candidate what he or she finds satisfying in a job. In order to do this effectively, you first need to have a clear picture of what the job has to offer—both intrinsic and extrinsic factors.

Use the worksheet shown in Table 8-2 to help develop a list of factors that you want to cover during the job-fit interview. Keep in mind that you're not looking for positive and negative aspects of the job. There are no such things. What you see as a positive someone else may see as a negative.

✔ Most Important	Factor	Comments
	Variety (same task every day, job rotation, multitasking required)	
	Autonomy (very little autonomy, very little supervision)	
	Feedback (customer feedback, quality checks on own work, track own sales figures)	
	Part vs. Whole (assembly line vs. cells, up-front sales vs. start-to-finish sales)	
	Interaction with Co-workers (teams, individual, both)	
	Work Environment (office, plant, warehouse, outdoors, temperature and cleanliness, physical requirements, safety issues)	
	Compensation (commission, salary, hourly, bonuses, pay-for-performance vs. seniority, rate of pay)	
	Growth Opportunities (on-the-job training, promotional opportunities)	
	Supervisory Style (traditional vs. empowering)	
	Work Schedule (shifts, shift rotation, hours/day, hours/week, overtime, weekend work, flex time)	
	Benefits (health, retirement, day care)	
	Location (transportation, parking)	
	Job Stability (company's financial status and reputation in community)	
	Other	

Table 8-2. Worksheet for determining motivational job factors

Why They Leave

At an automotive manufacturing firm in the Midwest, the HR explained why some employees would leave the company despite excellent working conditions, great pay and benefits, and a very empowering style of supervision. He told about a man and a woman who had just left the company. Both were great employees: they worked hard, never complained about overtime, learned different positions quickly, and could rotate between a wide range of stations without making mistakes. They left after a little less than nine months.

The man was almost in tears because he said that everyone had treated him so well and he really enjoyed building cars. The problem was that he grew up on a farm and could never get used to working inside all day long. He said that he had lost about 15 pounds since he started at the plant because he was so uncomfortable and wasn't sleeping or eating well.

The woman had worked as an elementary school teacher for two years before joining the company. She enjoyed working at the plant, the training, her co-workers, and her pay. However, she was going to take a cut in pay of almost 50% and go back to teaching because she just couldn't get used to the repetitive pace of the production line.

The company got nine good months from these two employees. But that's not as good as it seems. Consider the following points. New hires get five weeks of formal training and conditioning before they step onto the line. It takes about two months before most employees are proficient in more than two workstations. Consequently, most errors and accidents occur within the first six months of employment. So, losing someone within nine months creates some real problems for productivity, safety, and quality.

Different people will find certain aspects of the job more or less rewarding. For example, a sales position may offer a small base salary plus commission and require 80% travel. This will appeal to some people and be unacceptable to others. So try to be objective: list all factors that may affect motivational fit. Then, go back and check the factors that you feel will be the most important determinants of motivational fit.

Then, develop a few interview questions to target the items on your list. For instance, if the position requires working in dirty conditions, you may want to ask, "Tell me about the hardest and dirtiest job you ever had. What did you like most about it? What did you like least?" Make your questions as open-ended as possible and ask the candidate to explain or elaborate on his or her answers. For example, if the job offers a unique type of compensation plan, you might ask, "What type of compensation would most interest you?" In this case, you would want to focus not only on how much the candidate was interested in making but also how he or she would like to be paid. Follow up by asking why the candidate would prefer a particular approach over another.

You don't need to ask a question about every single factor. In many cases, you can ask some general questions that will help you gain a better understanding of the candidate's motivational fit. Some common interview questions for evaluating motivational fit are presented in Table 8-3.

You'll notice that these questions are very open-ended, not "yes or no" questions. Open-ended questions allow the candidate to open up, to talk freely. It's best to start with open-ended questions and save your more focused questions for later. An example of a focused question is: "This job pays a base salary of X and then pays based on commission. What are your thoughts about that approach? Are you comfortable with it?"

The problem with using focused questions early on is that they can open up a "selling process" that tends to shape the content of the information. If you start with a focused question that reveals what the job has to offer, the candidate may be tempted to give the desirable response—whether or not it accurately reflects what he or she finds satisfying or motivating. This is particularly true when the position is highly desirable for one reason or another. On the other hand, if the position is hard to fill, the interviewer may be tempted to try to "sell" a skilled candidate on the job by asking focused ques-

Lead Question	Follow-up Questions
Tell me about the types of activities you've done on the job over the past two years.	Which tasks did you enjoy doing the most? What did you least enjoy?
Tell me about the best jobs you've ever had.	What did you like most about them? What didn't you like about them?
Tell me what you'd like about this job. [Note: This is usually not a great question but will help you get a feel for how the candidate's expectations are align with what the job offers.]	Why would you like these aspects of the job? What would you like least and why?
Have you ever worked as a [target position] before? Tell me what you liked most about it. Tell me what you liked least about it.	Why did you leave that job? What would interest you in a similar position?
Which would you prefer: to be paid a stable monthly salary or to put some of your salary at risk, based on your performance?	Why? Have you ever worked with that type of compensation package? How did it turn out?

Table 8-3. Sample motivational fit interview questions

tions that build up the positive aspects of the job. In either case, motivational fit is overlooked.

You may be able to "sell" the job or be "sold" on the candidate, but the question is, will you be satisfied with the "sale"? Remember: if the candidate is not truly a good fit for the job, it's unlikely that he or she will be a productive, long-term employee.

Other Means of Evaluating Motivational Fit

In addition to evaluating motivational fit via the interview, there are other tools that can help you gain a perspective on a candidate's motivational fit—vocational interest inventories, customized motivational-fit questionnaires, and a realistic job preview followed by brief interviews.

Vocational Interest Inventories

Vocational interest inventories are self-report tests. They ask the candidate to respond to a series of questions or statements for which there is really no right or wrong answer. There are a number of commercially available interest inventories that provide feedback regarding which types of jobs would be the most appropriate for a person. Although interest inventories are generally used by vocational counselors in educational settings to help people find careers that match their interests, they can provide valuable insights for employers.

First Focus on Fit

If you decide to assess motivational fit during the interview, we suggest that you do it first. If the candidate is a good fit, then gather information on his or her skills, abilities, and education. If not, then you may want to end the interview at that point. Motivational fit is that important! And, you'll save time (both yours and the candidate's) and resources by eliminating unsuitable candidates early in the process.

Although an interest inventory may not provide you with an exact recommendation for a particular type of position, it may provide valuable information about the general types of positions that would best fit the candidate. You could then extrapolate to the position in question.

For instance, the inventory may tell you that this person would be most appropriate for working in a coaching or teaching role. If you're filling a consultant position that requires a high level of interaction with clients, explaining your company's products or services, then this might be a good fit. In other cases, the inventory may provide feedback that directly relates to the target position (e.g., sales).

Customized Motivational-Fit Questionnaires

Some companies have been very successful developing questionnaires for positions that typically are associated with high turnover. There are two general approaches to customized motivational-fit questionnaires.

One approach is to provide candidates with a list of work activities—some involved in the particular job and some not. Candidates are asked to rate how interested they would be in performing those activities. Sometimes, they're asked to rank them. The questionnaires are scored by looking at how candidates rate or rank the activities involved in the job. If they show no particular interest in a number of activities that are part of the job, then it's likely they won't enjoy performing the job. Figure 8-1 shows a sample of this type of questionnaire.

A related approach is to present a series of pairs of job characteristics that people would generally find comparable in desirability. One of these characteristics describes the target position; the other does not. The candidate is asked which characteristic he or she would prefer. As with the previous approach, if the candidate tends to favor characteristics that are not part of the job over those that are, this might indicate a poor fit. The example shown in Figure 8-2 illustrates this approach.

As with any customized test, these inventories need to be validated in some manner. There's more on this in Chapter 9.

Pros and Cons of Vocational Interest Inventories and Customized Questionnaires

Both of these methods have a number of real strengths, and each has its own weakness.

The primary weakness of the vocational interest inventories is that they can be overly general and not provide enough specific information about the target position. For instance, sales positions differ greatly depending on the product or service being sold, the level of interaction with the customer, and the philosophy of the company. These differences may not be covered by the inventory.

A weakness of the customized questionnaire is that it requires more time and effort to develop than to use a commercially available inventory. Also, most customized questionnaires focus on a small number of positions and aren't appropriate for a broad range of positions.

Read each statement and rate it in terms of how interested you would be in performing the activity on a regular basis. Use the following scale:

1	**2**	**3**
Not Willing or Interested	Willing but Not Really Interested	Definitely Willing and Interested

1. Talk on the telephone with customers for seven hours per day.

2. Try to convince people to purchase your company's products.

3. Work closely with co-workers.

4. Answer questions that people have about your company's products.

(*Note that items 1 and 4 are actually part of the job, whereas items 2 and 3 are not.*)

Figure 8-1. A questionnaire to rate enjoyment of job activities

Read each pair of job statements and select which type of job you would prefer. Indicate your preference by using the scale below:

1	**2**	**3**
Definitely Prefer Job A	Neutral	Definitely Prefer Job B

Job A
A job that requires you to work closely with other co-workers to achieve goals.

Job B
A job in which you will work by yourself on projects with little interaction with co-workers.

Figure 8-2. An example of a paired characteristics question

A major strength of both these approaches is that they can be administered to a large number of candidates. Those who clearly don't fit the profile can be screened out before the interview stage. Also, like other tests, they tend to be very reliable and the scoring is consistent from one person to another. They can also provide outstanding information for use in the interview. The interviewer can follow up on some of the more critical ratings by the candidate. In any case, used effectively, these tools can really help you make decisions about motivational fit.

Realistic Job Previews as a Starting Point

A lot of companies use realistic job previews (RJPs) to provide candidates with an opportunity to see what the job has to offer. You'll remember from Chapter 5 that an RJP should present the job accurately. Some aspects of the job may be appealing to certain people and others may be unappealing.

In Chapter 5 we discussed how to present an RJP during a screening phone interview. A more thorough RJP (often, in the form of a brief video) can be presented during the orientation on the day candidates go through the testing/interview process. The RJP is intended to serve as a screening tool in that candidates are encouraged to think about whether or not the job is right for them and decide if they want to continue with the selection process. Therefore, the RJP is most effective when it's not used to sell the job.

You can make the RJP a much more effective screening tool by including a short, yet focused interview after the preview. This is a great time to candidly

TRICKS OF THE TRADE

A Starting Point

The RJP cannot replace an evaluation of motivational fit. It will raise as many questions as it answers. But it provides a great starting point for talking about the job.

answer candidates' questions, discuss which aspects of the job they liked and which they didn't, and clarify any aspects of the RJP that needs elaboration.

But No One Really Wants to Do This Job!

What if there isn't much to enjoy in the position you're trying to fill?

Are you ever going to find a candidate who says, "Wow, this is exactly what I've always wanted to do!" Maybe not. But let me give you an example that reinforces the idea that moti-

---

Workin' in a Mine

Would you like to work in a mine? Miners routinely work hundreds of feet below the earth's surface and rarely see the sun. Although there are a lot of safety procedures, there is always the chance of a catastrophic accident that could collapse the mine and trap dozens of miners. At first glance, not the most desirable position.

Well, we were working with a company in southern Indiana to help hire production team members for a new manufacturing plant. We were talking with a local recruiter and reviewing some job applications. A number of candidates had prior mining experience and were now applying for jobs at the plant.

The recruiter told us that he'd hired lots of miners, and they make great employees. They're reliable, learn quickly, and work hard. The only drawback is that whenever a new mine opens up anywhere in the area and begins hiring, they immediately return to the mines. He said it was in their blood. They just couldn't wait to get back underground!

---

vational fit is important for any job.

Remember that there are a lot of factors that influence whether a person will enjoy a job. While you may or may not find people who have "in their blood" a desire to do the work you're hiring for, there are undoubtedly people who feel that the pros outweigh the cons. You'll be much better off if you try to identify such people than if you just assume that no one really wants to do the job.

What About College Students and Part-time Employees?

A lot of companies, particularly in the service sector, have found success hiring college students to work part-time. Companies like Starbucks Coffee are routinely staffed by students working their way through college or graduate school. Clearly, these students aren't looking for a long-term career serving coffee. But remember the matter of intrinsic and extrinsic factors. While making cappuccinos may not provide intrinsic intellectual challenges, the coffeehouse provides flexible schedules and an opportunity to earn a decent wage in a relatively low-stress environment (as well as cheap access to caffeine!).

The key points discussed in this chapter can also apply to part-time and student employees. Some will be more inclined to work in coffee shops, while others will prefer to work in warehouses or on production lines. Keep an open and candid dialogue going with these candidates during the interview process and acknowledge that this will not be a long-term job. Try to determine, however, whether the position fits what the person wants in a job at this time. If the fit is good, you've got a great chance of hiring an excellent employee.

Manager's Checklist for Chapter 8

❑ Make evaluating motivational fit a priority in your hiring process. Motivational fit is a more important factor than skills and abilities in hiring people who will be satisfied with a job and stay with it.

❑ Evaluate the key intrinsic and extrinsic factors of the job. Determine for each factor what the job offers and what it doesn't. In a motivational-fit evaluation, give more weight to the intrinsic than to the extrinsic.

❑ Determine motivational fit before assessing skills and abilities. Hiring candidates based on ability without assessing motivational fit will cost the company in the long run.

❑ Develop some interview questions that will help you compare the candidate's expectations with what the job offers.

❑ Depending on the type of position and the number of candidates, you may wish to consider alternative methods of evaluating motivational fit—vocational interest inventories, customized motivational-fit questionnaires, and a realistic job preview followed by brief interviews.

How to Use Testing

Terri is the HR manager at a 1,000-person manufacturing facility. Over the past 9 months the plant has been going through an expansion, hiring over 200 new employees and expecting to hire another 200 over the next 12 months. In addition, last year the plant shifted from single production lines to a work team format that puts more responsibility on the production associates.

Terri and the plant manager are frustrated, however, with the quality of the new hires and the performance of employees who have been there for years. There's a lot more scrap and downtime than they ever expected, and most associates are lagging far behind schedule in terms of cross-training, which greatly affects productivity and quality.

Since the plant started up four years ago, Terri has been using a lengthy selection process that requires all applicants to take a 3-hour basic skills test (reading, basic math, and general intelligence) and then go through two 1-hour interviews with the hiring manager and the HR manager. The process had worked well, providing good employees—prior to this change in the work design.

The requirements of the job have changed with the move to work teams. The profile of the successful employee has changed, and the testing approach in use now, although quite time-consuming, does not adequately evaluate key areas of success. Terri needs to reevaluate the profile of the successful team member and set up testing to cover those areas.

In this chapter, you will learn how to tailor your testing approach based on the job's profile for success. This chapter covers the following topics:

- Selection systems as stock portfolios
- How do I know that this test works?
- What types of tests are there?
- Tests vs. interviews: pros and cons
- Bang for the buck: getting the most from your tests

Selection Systems as Stock Portfolios

Although at first blush it looks like quite a stretch, there's actually a lot of similarity between testing systems and stock portfolios. Why?

Well, think of individual tests as being similar to individual stocks or even individual mutual funds. Would it be a good idea to put all of your money into a single stock or a single mutual fund? Probably not. The primary reason is that your risk level would be too high, especially over the long term, and you would be unlikely to meet your investment goals.

This is very similar to using a single test or interview to select your employees. Your risk of hiring the wrong person increases because you can't possibly cover all of the relevant competency areas with a single test.

This analogy with stocks is a good way to think about testing because most managers understand the logic of portfolio diversification. Let's consider an example that should help strengthen the similarities.

Let's say that you've identified five competency areas that make up the successful profile of a production team member (Figure 9-1). It would be nice if there were one test that could

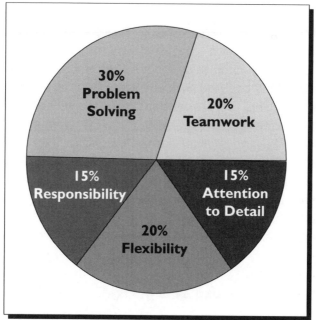

Figure 9-1. Sample profile for production team members

cover all of these areas, but that's not realistic. Instead, we should look at putting together a portfolio of tests or interviews that will effectively cover these competencies. Table 9-1 shows a sample portfolio for evaluating these areas.

	Personality Inventory	Identifying Differences Test	Critical Thinking Test	Situational Judgment Test	Interview
Teamwork	30%			40%	30%
Problem Solving			40%	40%	20%
Attention to Detail	30%	70%			
Flexibility	70%				30%
Responsibility	80%				20%

Table 9-1. Sample selection portfolio for production associates

There are some key things to notice in that portfolio. Across the top of the table are four types of tests and an interview that could be used to evaluate the five competencies. We'll discuss individual tests in more detail later in the chapter. For now let's assume that each is a distinct type of test.

In the columns are percentages that show how much weight to give that particular test or interview when calculating an overall rating for that competency. For example, to come up with a final score for teamwork, we would give equal weight to the personality test and the interview (30% each) and slightly more to the situational judgment test (40%). Not every cell in the table contains a percentage. That's because some tests don't work well for evaluating those competencies.

As you can see, we don't measure any competencies with only one single test or interview. Think of this as "diversifying our portfolio," not putting all of our eggs in one basket. The most important reason for diversifying is that no single test or interview is a perfect predictor of any single competency. Combining several approaches helps to cover the competency more completely. In terms of the stock portfolio analogy, this is like holding some blue-chip stocks, some small caps, some bonds, and some international stocks. The philosophy of diversification and increased coverage is very similar. Over the long run, you're better off using a small, yet diversified group of good tests to help you make decisions, rather than basing your decision on just one test.

> **TRICKS OF THE TRADE**
>
> ## Testing, 1, 2, 3...
>
> Although diversifying your coverage of the competency areas improves your chances of making a good hiring decision, don't use too many tests. A good rule of thumb would be to try to evaluate a competency in two places and no more than three. Using too many tests for a competency makes it difficult to combine the results in a meaningful manner.

How Do I Know That This Test Works?

One of the first things you learn in an advanced testing course is that there's no such thing as a valid test. Wow! Pretty strong statement. Let's take a look at what this statement means.

You've probably heard of the term *test validity*. When we talk about test validity, we're actually referring to the inferences or conclusions we make about the test for a given purpose or use. A test may be considered valid for one use or application and invalid for another.

Drawing the Right Conclusions

Let's say that we have a test that measures the ability to solve complex mathematical problems. We know that this test is a good predictor of how people will perform in advanced mathematics courses and fields such as engineering and physics. Is it a valid test? Well, yes and no. It's probably valid in helping to select engineers, physicists, and mathematicians, but it's a terrible test for hiring janitors!

We should think of test validity in terms of how appropriate a test is for a particular use. It's not the *test* that is valid or invalid, but the *inferences* or *conclusions* we draw from it.

Smart Managing

Validity

What do we mean by validity? It's a matter of how appropriate a test is for our specific purposes. Is it appropriate for hiring managers? What about for engineers? An appropriate test will yield valid conclusions. There are really three types of validity that are important for testing purposes: content, construct, and criterion.

There's a simple way to think about test validity. In selecting or promoting employees, we want an answer to a simple question: Do people who do better on this test perform better on the job? A simple question, but how do you answer it? One of the best ways is to conduct a *validation study*.

Key Term

Content validity A measure of how well the content of the test corresponds to the content and requirements of the job. Many tests of knowledge are content valid because they ask questions about things you need to know to perform the job. Questions about electricity, voltage, and circuits would likely be valid content for a test to evaluate how much an electrician knows about electricity.

Construct validity A measure of how well a test assesses intelligence or extroversion or shyness. Such areas, called constructs, are more difficult to assess than content. A test of teamwork would be considered construct valid if it accurately evaluated the ability to interact effectively with others.

Criterion validity A measure of the link between test results and job performance. If people who score higher on the test perform better on the job than people with lower test scores, the test is said to have criterion validity. That means it's a predictor of job performance. It's possible for a test to have high criterion validity even if we don't know exactly what the test measures, that is, if there's low construct validity. With criterion validity, what the test measures is irrelevant; all that matters is that those who score high on the test also perform well on the job.

Although a predictive study may seem superior to a concurrent study, the difference is actually insignificant for two reasons: one, it's almost impossible to conduct a pure predictive study; and two, research has shown that the results turn out the same for both types of studies.

If you're considering using a test or a group of tests in making a hiring decision, you have three options for determining the validity or appropriateness of the tests for your specific purpose.

Option 1. Conduct a validation study. This is the most complicated of the three options. But, if done properly, it will provide you with the best evidence of how well the test will work for your situation. To be effective, validation studies require testing a fairly large number of individuals (60 to 100+). They

> **Validation study** An investigation that compares scores on a test or tests with important, on-the-job performance measures. The study will result in a mathematical index of the strength of the relationship between these two, such as a correlation coefficient or a hit-rate percentage. Typically, validation studies fall into one of two categories: concurrent studies or predictive studies.
>
> **Concurrent study** A validation study using employees who are already performing the job. We give current employees the test(s) and see how the results relate to their job performance.
>
> **Predictive study** A validation study using candidates for the job. Candidates are tested and hired (ideally, not using scores from the test as part of the hiring decision). Then, at some time in the future, we compare their test scores with their job performance.

also require some type of reliable and accurate measure of job performance to compare the test with (e.g., supervisory ratings, attendance records, turnover data, sales performance). You should also seek the help of someone familiar with conducting validation studies and statistical analyses, such as an industrial psychologist. This solution is appropriate for companies that are interviewing a large number of employees for a small group of positions. A company that hires several hundred salespeople would benefit greatly from a validation study.

Option 2. Generalize from previous studies. Sometimes you're not able to conduct a validation study. For example, if you're opening a new plant, there's no way to determine how well the test performs in your facility before you actually hire all (or at least many) of your employees. Also, if there are only a few people in the position, the sample size will be too small to allow any meaningful interpretation of the analysis.

In these situations, you can evaluate how well the test has performed in situations similar to yours. Test publishers or consultants should be able to provide you with information on the validity of their tests for different positions. Keep in mind the analogy between stocks and tests: past performance is no guarantee of future performance. But if the test has shown a consistent pattern of validity for similar positions, then you can feel relatively comfortable that it will suit your purpose.

Option 3. Evaluate the content validity of the test. For some tests, such as tests of knowledge, evaluating content validity is the best way to determine the appropriateness of a test. When you evaluate the content validity of a test you should:

1. Gather a group of job content experts (JCEs) to evaluate the content of the test items. Supervisors of the position usually make very good JCEs for this purpose.

2. Have the JCEs evaluate each test item and evaluate how relevant it is to the target position. They should focus on these two questions: Do people in the position need to know the information asked for

> **Key Term**
>
> **Job Content Experts (JCEs)** People knowledgeable about the content of the job and its requirements.

in this question? If so, is the level of difficulty equal to the level required in the position? For example, an electrical technician may need to know about fundamental electrical theory, but not at the same level as an electrical engineer.

3. Try to eliminate items that are not judged relevant. Either don't score them or delete them from the test.

> **Mistake Proofing**
>
> **Evaluating Validity**
> When you evaluate the validity of a test or review earlier validation studies, pay close attention to the validation criteria. For example, when a validation study concludes that a certain test can predict job performance, find out exactly how the researchers measured job performance. In some instances, researchers simply ask the candidates to rate their own performance on the job! Appropriate criteria should include ratings of performance from someone other than the candidate, such as a supervisor, or more objective measures, such as attendance or actual sales vs. sales goals.

	Conducting a Validity Study	Generalizing from Similar Validity Studies	Evaluating Content Validity
Strengths	• Best indicator for your particular position • Better able to set cutoff scores and predict performance levels	• Easy to gather information from previous studies • Able to see how consistently a test has performed in multiple settings	• Relatively easy to establish • Ensures that test covers important job-related content
Weaknesses	• Most difficult and costly to conduct • Need professional assistance • Requires relatively large sample size	• Never sure if it will work in your particular setting • Differences in job content between your position and the previous implementations could reduce validity	• Harder to establish cutoffs than other methods • Don't really know if it's a good predictor of performance
Most Appropriate Uses	• Large-scale hiring for one to four general positions or job groupings	• Testing where number of positions or jobs is high relative to number of people employed in them	• Test of knowledge • Situations where the link between content of test and content of job is clear and well defined

Table 9-2. Appropriateness of methods for determining test validity

4. Document your process for determining the relevancy of the test.

A quick summary of the different approaches to determining whether a test is valid or not is provided in Table 9-2.

Understanding Correlation and Statistical Significance

The results of a validity study will often be summarized by a *validity coefficient* or a *correlation coefficient*. Correlation coefficients are numbers ranging between −1 and +1.

A negative correlation means that as one variable gets larger, the other variable gets smaller. For example, the faster your computer, the less time it takes to run a program. So, speed and time are negatively correlated.

A positive correlation means that as one variable becomes larger, so does the other variable. For example, taller people

Range in Validity Coefficient	Strength of Relationship between Predictor and Criteria
r = .00 to .19	Little, if any, relationship
r = .20 to .29	Small to moderate relationship
r = .30 to .39	Fairly strong relationship
r = .40 to .59	Strong relationship
r = .60 and higher	Very strong relationship

Table 9-3. Ranges of validity coefficients

tend to have longer feet. So, height and shoe size are positively correlated.

When a correlation coefficient is used to measure validity, it's called a validity coefficient. The symbol for correlation coefficient is "r." This is sometimes written "r_{xy}," which means the correlation between X and Y (e.g., a test and job performance).

Table 9-3 will help you understand what levels of validity you can expect from tests.

In testing, correlations (or validities) of .60 and higher are very good. Obviously, a correlation of .60 is not a perfect correlation, so there are going to be times where what we predict doesn't actually turn out to be 100% correct. However, even modest validities (e.g., .20 to .30) can be helpful in terms of selecting employees. A good way to think of correlations is in terms of accuracy. The higher the correlation between two variables, such as a test and performance on the job, the more accurate our interpretations of the test score will be. Consider the following example to better understand how validity relates to decision-making accuracy.

Let's assume that we're going to try a new method for hiring production team members. There are three tests that we can use to select these employees. There are already 500 team members in the facility. To pilot-test the three tests, we take a sample of 100 team members, with varying performance records, and administer the tests to them. We also

Test	Correlation with Performance
Test 1	$r_{xy} = .62*$
Test 2	$r_{xy} = .37*$
Test 3	$r_{xy} = .23*$

gather performance ratings from their team leaders and group leaders on a 10-point scale, ranging from much less than acceptable to outstanding. We correlate the scores on the three tests with the performance ratings and get the results shown in the chart above.

If we compare these correlations with the interpretation guidelines shown in Table 9-3, we see that test 1 performed extremely well, test 2 performed well, and test 3 performed moderately at best. The asterisk (*) next to each correlation shows that they're all statistically significant. You'll often hear the phrase, "…the results were statistically significant," but what does this really mean?

Statistical significance means, in simple terms, that you're unlikely to get a result of this value due simply to chance. A significance level is assigned to the finding, which tells you how likely it would be to happen just because of chance. Usually a level of 95% is considered acceptable. This means that we're 95% confident that the results did not occur just because of chance. This is usually written as "$p<.05$," meaning that there is less than a 5% chance that the results were due to chance.

One of the drawbacks of statistical significance

Statistical significance
A term indicating that a result is not likely due to chance. Significance is measured in terms of a percentage. Usually a level of 95% is considered acceptable. This means that we are 95% confident that the results did not occur just by chance. This is usually written as "$p<.05$," meaning that there's less than a 5% possibility that the results occurred just by chance.

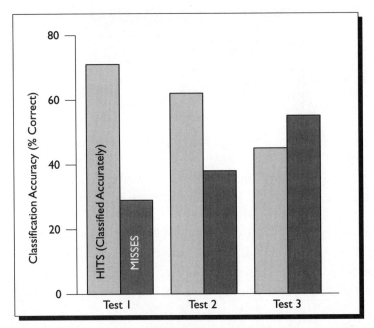

Figure 9-2. Comparative classification accuracy of three tests

is that it is greatly influenced by sample size. For example, a correlation of .50 based on a sample of 20 would not be statistically significant, but a correlation of .05 would be significant with a sample of 2,000. So, statistical significance does not mean that there is a strong relationship between the two variables; it just means that the results are reliable.

Perhaps a better way of considering the differences in validity would be to see how accurately the three tests predict job performance as acceptable or less than acceptable. Figure 9-2 shows the accuracy of the three tests (based on a simulated set of data). A *hit* means that a test accurately classified the person and a *miss* means that it was wrong.

Notice that test 3 makes more misses than hits! Even though the correlation coefficient is statistically significant (.23), this test has little validity in this situation.

Now let's compare test 1 and test 2. The validity coefficient for test 1 (.62) is 40% greater than for test 2 (.37). This is a fairly big difference. But even more impressive is the difference in "net accuracy of prediction" (hits-to-misses) between the two tests. The net accuracy with test 1 is 42, but only 24 with test 2. We get 75% greater net accuracy of prediction by using test 1 instead of test 2! The moderate difference in validity results in a dramatic increase in accuracy of prediction.

What Types of Tests Are There?

Tests measure all types of things. In general, there are three broad categories:

- **Skill or Ability Tests.** These measure some basic talent, such as general mathematical ability, problem-solving skills, and mechanical reasoning. They are really designed to assess an ability to do something.
- **Personality or Interest Inventories.** These are called *inventories* rather than *tests* because they identify characteristics, rather than measuring according to a certain standard.
- **Knowledge Tests.** These measure a level of understanding in a specific area. These tests are often used in certification exams.

Is any of these test types better than the others? It all depends on your purpose. The question you should always ask is, "Will the information I get from this test help me hire better employees?" Table 9-4 (page 146) compares the three categories of tests.

As we discussed in the first section of this chapter, you don't need to choose the "best" test to cover everything. For most positions, it's likely that skill, personality, and knowledge combine to define successful performers. So, you'd likely use all three types of test to evaluate candidates.

Tests vs. Interviews: Pros and Cons

Let's say that you've done a job analysis and know that a successful salesperson at your company needs to be outgoing, organized, very flexible, able to build a solid relationship with customers, and able to handle rejection. Why would you use a

	Skill & Ability Tests	Personality Inventories	Knowledge Tests
General Description	Require some level of skill or ability. There are right or wrong answers.	Provides candidates with statements that they typically agree or disagree with. There are no right or wrong answers.	Require a general understanding of key content. There are right and wrong answers.
Key Question It Answers	"Does this person have the appropriate skill or ability to actually DO something?"	"Does this person have the characteristics or general profile that we are looking for?"	"Does this person know what he or she should know to be successful in this job?"
Most Appropriate Uses	When a particular ability or skill is required for success on the job. Work best for cognitive competencies such as general problem solving and logical reasoning.	When components other than knowledge or skill influence performance on the job.	When some type of specific knowledge greatly impacts job performance.

Table 9-4. Comparison of three categories of tests

test to evaluate candidates for these characteristics, rather than just interviewing around them? Think about the stock portfolio analogy again. Would you put all your money into one single stock, no matter how good? Probably not. Then why make your selection decision based entirely on an interview, even a good one?

It's not just the logic of diversification. There are other reasons for using tests to replace interviews, or at least to supplement them.

Advantages of Tests vs. Interviews

There are a variety of advantages of tests over interviews for you to consider in evaluating candidates.

- **Tests tend to be more reliable**. Because tests are standardized, all candidates answer the same questions and their responses are scored consistently. Test scores tend to be more reliable than interview scores because tests use objective scoring procedures, while interview scores are influenced by the subjectivity of the interviewer.

- **Tests allow us to evaluate complex competencies without formal training**. Are you a good evaluator of a person's work ethic or the ability to solve complex problems? Maybe so, but are you sure that all of the people who will be doing interviews are just as good? A well-designed test allows us to gather reliable and accurate information that might be difficult to gather effectively through an interview.
- **Tests can help to reduce the time you spend in interviews**. Why spend an hour in an interview with a candidate who clearly doesn't fit the profile to do the job well? Tests can screen out unacceptable candidates efficiently, so you can spend your time interviewing candidates who are more likely to succeed on the job.

Advantages of Interviews vs. Tests

There are some areas where interviews clearly have advantages over tests.

- **Interviews are often perceived to be more fair than tests.** Despite the objective reliability of tests, most people, including candidates, view interviews as being a fairer method of determining who gets the job. Why? Maybe because candidates feel they have a greater sense of control in making their case with a person.
- **Interviews provide face-to-face opportunity.** It's always a good idea to meet and talk with a candidate before you hire him or her. Whether or not it helps you make a more accurate decision, it sure makes you feel more comfortable with your decision.
- **Interviews allow for follow-up questions.** Tests don't usually provide an opportunity for candidates to explain their answers in more detail. In an

> **Don't Undertest**
> A lot of companies interview too much and test too little. Interviews are easy to do and allow you to cover a lot of areas, including abilities, skills, personality types, and technical knowledge. But that doesn't mean that they're giving you good information. The interview is a valuable tool, but it has limitations.

interview, you can ask for explanations and probe for details.

It's really not a question of whether interviews are better than tests, or vice versa. The most comprehensive selection systems use both tests and interviews to evaluate candidates and make decisions. In fact, it's not a bad idea to evaluate the same competency area with both tests and interviews. For instance, if you are selecting salespeople, you might want to use a personality inventory to get information on the candidates' work ethic and general interpersonal style, and how organized they are, and use a measure of logical reasoning to evaluate their problem-solving skills. You may also want to interview around interpersonal skills and their ability to interact with potential customers, as well as their planning and organizing skills. Tests and interviews can form a powerful combination and allow you to make a more accurate and reliable decision than you could by using either one by itself.

Bang for the Buck: Getting the Most from Your Tests

Let's say that you've identified some tests that will provide accurate and reliable information about some key areas that are important for success on the job. You've reviewed the technical reports, and they indicate that these tests are valid predictors of performance. The validity (a.k.a. *accuracy*) of the tests is very high (.70), so you know they work. You've set the cutoff on the test at a point such that 90% of all candidates pass the cutoff and are then hired.

Guess what? The return on investment (ROI) for that extremely accurate test is probably very low! Why? Because the cutoff is set so low that you're not screening effectively. So, you're hiring people who aren't successful in the job.

ROI (or *utility*) of selection systems is based on three factors:

1. The percentage of people in the general population (or at least in your applicant pool) who can perform the job successfully
2. The test's ability to predict performance (its validity)

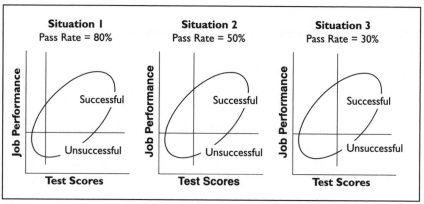

Figure 9-3. Differences in ROI for three cutoff scores

3. The cutoff levels you use for selecting employees

Figure 9-3 shows how your cutoff score can affect your ROI. It depicts three situations: factors 1 and 2 remain the same, but factor 3 varies.

The candidate pool is the same in each situation. The validity of the tests is also exactly the same. The relationship between test scores and job performance is not perfect. If it were, the actual candidate scores would fall on a straight diagonal line. As it is, the scores form a diagonal, elliptical cluster. The performance standards (successful or unsuccessful) are demarcated by the horizontal line.

The only variable is the cutoff, indicated by the vertical line. Candidates to the right of this line will be hired and those to the left will not. In the first situation, the cutoff score is set fairly low, so 80% of the candidates pass. In the second situation, the cutoff score is set a little higher: 50% pass the test. In the third situation, the cutoff score is set even higher, so only 30% pass the test.

But how does the cutoff relate to ROI? To answer that question, let's look at the portion of each graph that shows candidates who are hired

> **Know the Score**
>
> **T**RICKS **OF THE** **T**RADE
>
> Setting appropriate cutoff scores is important. The results of a validation study should help you determine where you want to set the cutoff point.

(the area within the ellipse that is to the right of the vertical line). Some of the people hired were successful (the area above the horizontal line), and some were unsuccessful (the area below the horizontal line). Obviously, you want more successful hires than unsuccessful hires.

How do the cutoff scores affect this ratio?

In the first example, with lower cutoff scores and an 80% pass rate, the ratio of successful and unsuccessful hires is about 50/50. In other words, if you use this cutoff score, 50% of your hires will be successful and 50% will not. Considering that you can get these same odds by flipping a coin, your ROI would be very low with this cutoff.

In the second example, with a higher cutoff score and a 50% pass rate, the ratio is about 60/40: six out of every ten hires will be successful. Your ROI has slightly increased by a small increase in the cutoff score.

In the third example, with the highest cutoff score and the lowest pass rate, the ratio is about 80/20. Now eight out of every ten hires will be successful (a 20% miss rate). A higher cutoff dramatically increases the utility (ROI) of the tests.

This example shows how a higher cutoff point will increase the likelihood of making successful hires. There are, however, other factors to consider when determining the cutoff score and evaluating the ROI of the test:

- The cost of recruitment
- The quality of the applicant pool
- The adverse impact of specific cutoff scores on protected groups
- The difference in performance between good and poor employees

For instance, if the applicant pool is small, a very high cutoff could prolong the hiring process, because so many applicants would fail. In this case, you'd want to weigh the costs of the hiring process if you set the cutoff high against the costs resulting from lower performance if you set the cutoff low.

Manager's Checklist for Chapter 9

❑ You'll make more informed hiring decisions if you use a small yet diversified number of good tests.

❑ Consider the competencies in your job analysis (Chapter 1) and realistically determine whether you can effectively cover them with an interview. (If your answer is always yes, then you're not being realistic.)

❑ Determine which types of tests would be the most useful for you. No single test can cover all areas.

❑ The validity of a test is determined by the usefulness of its conclusions. Determine the appropriateness of a test by conducting a concurrent or predictive validation study.

❑ Determine how you will interpret the information you get from the test and how you will combine it with information from other tests or from interviews.

❑ Use information from the job analysis, validation studies, and the test's norms to set cutoff scores that balance the needs of hiring the best employees, effectively using your applicant pool, and minimizing adverse impact.

❑ The key criterion when you consider a test is whether the information you would get from it would help you hire better employees.

❑ The most comprehensive selection systems use both tests and interviews to evaluate candidates and make decisions.

❑ Tests should be an integral part of most selection processes because they are generally accurate and reliable and can allow more effective and efficient evaluation than an interview.

Background Checks

Baxter Compounds, Inc., was dealing with a serious problem. During a minor disagreement on the job, Michael—a recent hire—assaulted Henry, a fellow team member. Soon after the incident, it was learned that Michael had a criminal history involving violence. The plant manager, the shift supervisor, and the human resources manager met to discuss the situation.

The plant manager was still in a state of shock. "I can't believe this happened. How could we let this happen?"

"Well, we fired Michael on the spot," said the supervisor. "Let's just hope that Henry is OK."

"And," added the HR manager, "that he doesn't sue us."

Because of that one incident, they were suddenly forced to deal with the hassle of firing an employee and with some serious long-term consequences: Henry's injuries, the effect on employee morale, and a possible lawsuit. All because Baxter Compounds, Inc., did not do a thorough background check on an employee.

Although this example may be extreme, it has unfortunately become an increasingly common workplace occurrence and represents just one of the possible effects of not doing thorough background checks.

This chapter will cover the important but often neglected process of checking a potential hire's background and references. For all the money invested in recruiting, selecting, and training people, why would you ignore something so simple and as proven as a background check? Sure, it takes time. But it's time well spent because it pays off later. As we have learned, past behavior predicts future behavior.

This chapter addresses the following questions:
- Why should you do background checks?
- What job-relevant elements should you check?
- How do you verify the information?
- When should you do background checks?
- Should you do it yourself or use an agency?
- How do you interpret, use, and store the results?

Why Should You Do Background Checks?

The answer to this question just takes a little common sense—and perhaps a few statistics to back it up. Consider the following points:

- An inquiry conducted by a congressional subcommittee discovered that over 30 million people had gained employment by falsifying information on their résumés or applications.
- Research suggests that as many as one out of five applicants falsifies information on a résumé or application.
- Violence in the workplace is a disturbingly growing trend. So much so that the phrase "disgruntled employee" has become a common character description in the news.
- It's estimated that U.S. businesses lose over $50 billion each year as a result of employee crime. This figure is probably much higher; companies are reluctant to report crimes. And it's not just big businesses feeling the pain. A recent study by the Association of Fraud Examiners found that companies with fewer than 100 employees are the number 1 target of workplace crime. These crime trends will likely increase, given the prevalence of computer automation and easier access to sensitive information.

There are two main reasons to conduct background checks. The first has to do with the success of your company. One objective of every company is to hire people who will help the company—or at least not hinder it. Background checks can help you choose people who are most likely to help your company. Let's consider three examples.

- Vaughn told you during his interview that he was responsible for implementing a new production measure at G-Whiz, Inc., that significantly increased his productivity. In talking to his former supervisor, you learn that no such measure was ever implemented and that Vaughn was an average employee. Would you hire him?
- Sandy stated on her application that she was never convicted of a crime in the last ten years. You check court records and discover that Sandy was found guilty of shoplifting six years ago. Would you hire her?
- Karen put on her résumé that she received her nursing license (LPN) through the University of Pittsburgh. A call to the institution reveals that Karen never completed the practical work needed for accreditation. Would you hire her?

Of course, the answers to the above questions depend on the situation. Sandy and Karen clearly falsified information on their application and résumé, which could justifiably eliminate them from further consideration. These falsehoods would be particularly damning if Sandy were applying for a sales clerk position or if Karen were applying for a nursing position. It's a little different for Vaughn. It's possible that his supervisor was not aware of Vaughn's efforts. And he didn't say anything negative about Vaughn's performance. The information is just another piece of the puzzle.

The point here is that without background checks, you would not have learned any of this information. In all three cases, you've learned something that you might want to consider when asking yourself, "How likely is it that this person will help (or at least not hinder) the company?"

If you still aren't convinced that it's worth your time and effort to conduct background checks, you might be swayed by our second reason for doing them—to avoid a lawsuit. Courts have found employers liable when an incompetent employee, in the course of work, was responsible for causing a situation in which another person was subjected to harm. The other person could be another employee, a customer or client, or a member of the general public.

The employer becomes responsible when there was a documented condition in the background of the incompetent employee that made the harmful action a definite possibility. The belief is that the company would have known about this possibility if the representatives (managers like you) had exercised due diligence and conducted a thorough background check. Then, the employer could have prevented the harmful action by not hiring that individual. When a company fails to exercise due diligence, it's called *negligent hiring.*

Conducting a background check may seem obvious for some jobs. For example, it makes sense to do a criminal background check on a person applying for a law enforcement position or a position that involves

> **Negligent hiring** The responsibility of an employer when an employee harms somebody while working , as a result of being unfit for the job, and the employer knew or should have known about the condition.

working with young children. (Believe it or not, negligent hiring does occur even for these types of positions!) However, while not as obvious, it is just as important to do background checks for other types of jobs. Consider the following examples.

A tow truck driver who was assaulted by a postal employee in the parking lot is suing the U.S. Postal Office for $500,000. This case is going forward, despite a law that states the U.S. government cannot be held liable for assaults committed by its employees. If the federal government can't beat the charge of negligent hiring, do you think your company could?

A hotel night clerk used his key to gain access to a guest's room. He's now on trial for assault and the hotel is being sued for negligent hiring: the employee had been convicted of rape six years earlier. The hotel management had not felt that a background check for a minimum-wage employee was worth the $50 fee. How do you think management feels about it now?

Of course, doing a good background check cannot prevent misconduct. But, it does substantially mitigate your risk.

A background check is always a good idea in any selection system. Some candidates simply exaggerate their credentials, while others actually falsify information. When jobs are scarce, applicants may be tempted to embellish or fabricate their backgrounds to gain a competitive advantage. When jobs are plentiful, applicants may omit things from their backgrounds that have kept them from getting jobs in the past. So it always makes sense to check out your applicants.

What Job-Relevant Elements Should You Check?

Some people believe in verifying everything on a résumé or application. The idea is that any fabrication is grounds for immediate rejection. However, this approach is time-consuming and costly—and it may get you into trouble if you check areas that are not job-relevant. For example, why do a credit check on a person applying for a janitorial position? It's unlikely that the information relates to job performance.

The first step in doing any good background check is to develop a list of job-related information that you need to verify. The information you learned during your competency analysis (Chapter 1) will help you do this. Sticking to job-relevant areas serves two purposes:

- It keeps you out of hot water, because only job-related data can legally be used to make hiring decisions.
- It makes the person providing the reference more comfortable and thus more likely to help you. (We'll discuss that challenge later.)

In general, background checks serve two purposes: to verify information on the application or résumé or gained during the interview, and to gather additional information that perhaps the applicant did not want you to know.

There are three main types of background checks:

- **Checking references.** This involves talking with people who are familiar with the candidate's work history and asking appropriate questions that focus on gathering job-related information—information that will help you evaluate the candidate's fit for the position.
- **Checking credentials.** This involves verifying such things as educational degrees, certifications, and licenses, and possibly investigating such areas as criminal convictions and credit histories.
- **Checking training needs.** Knowing a candidate's strengths and weaknesses before you hire him or her can help you identify training needs. That can save time and energy and improve productivity in the long run. The best people to ask are past supervisors.

This chapter will focus on the most common types of background checks: references and credentials. However, when speaking with references about a candidate, you should keep in mind the benefit of also checking training needs.

Deciding Which Elements Are Job-Related

To determine what to check, use your job analysis as a guide—and some common sense. For example, if you're hiring a crane operator, it's wise to check licensure. If you're hiring for a position that involves handling money, you should conduct a credit check. This not only protects you from in-house loss, but also from actions taken by the candidate on your behalf. If you were a manager for a credit card

> **Know the Time Limits**
>
> *MISTAKE PROOFING!*
>
> Some background areas have time limits. For instance, criminal convictions can be considered for only up to ten years and credit histories for only up to seven years for positions earning less than $20,000 annually. We strongly recommend checking federal and state guidelines before you check records.

company, would you want to hire financial consultants who had terrible credit histories?

If, after careful consideration, you determine that a criminal check and/or a credit check are unnecessary in your situation, you should, at the very least, verify educational information and employment experiences. These areas are where applicants most often exaggerate or fabricate.

Credit Checks

The Federal Fair Credit Reporting Act, as well as other state and local laws, regulates all credit information. If a credit check is a condition of employment, this must be disclosed to the applicant. Moreover, the results of the search must be made available to the applicant, if requested.

Table 10-1 presents a list of "typical" things to check and also a "tougher" list, which would take more time to cover but yield more information.

Most of the items in Table 10-1 (except those involving credentials and degrees) are relevant to all jobs. However,

Typical	Tougher
• Diploma, GED, or other degrees • Licenses, certifications, and other credentials • Tenure/dates of employment • Position held • Basic responsibilities • Name and position of supervisor • Compensation upon departure	• Reason for leaving • Eligible for rehire • Description of performance (on a scale of I to I0, in relation to other workers) • Comparison to person now performing the job • How reliable/conscientious • Provide an example of outstanding behavior • Strengths and developmental needs • Read part of résumé or application and ask reference to verify accuracy • Reservations I should have about hiring him or her

Table 10-1. Recommended background items to verify

make sure that everything you check is related to the particular job for which you're hiring. By now, you've probably recognized a recurring theme in this book: if it's not job-related, it's not useful!

How Do You Verify the Information?

Once you've decided to conduct background checks and determined what you need to check out, you have one more decision to make, the most difficult—how do you do it?

Background checks must be done in a deliberate fashion. It's not enough to rely on letters of recommendation—especially those supplied by the applicant! What applicant is going to give you a letter with anything negative? Letters provide only

> ### Create a Checklist
> To ensure consistency and accuracy, develop a checklist. Use the information from the competency analysis (Chapter 1) and the application/résumé screening checklist (Chapter 4) to create it. This structures the information so you do not omit important information or stray into areas not job-related. This also ensures that every applicant will go through the same process—another recurring theme throughout this book! See Figure 10-1 for an example.

what the writer thinks is important—and what the applicant thinks will help get the job! You can't explore, so you're forced to draw conclusions—correct or not. To investigate an applicant's background, you must call references and institutions. If you ever imagined playing Colombo or Perry Mason, here's your chance. And, we'll tell you how to do it.

One thing to keep in mind when talking with past employers is that you need to use effective follow-up questions to explore areas of interest. This helps define the behaviors that interest you. A good question is, "Can you clarify that or provide an example?" This works in almost any situation. However, just remember to confine your questions to areas that are job-relevant.

Candidate Name:	Social Security No.:
Education Verification	
Educational institution:	Person contacted: Date verified:
Dates attended: Graduated (Yes/No)?:	Degree received:
Technical institution:	Person contacted: Date verified:
Dates attended: Graduated (Yes/No)?:	Degree received:
Criminal Record Search	
Type of record: Search results:	Period searched: County:
Employment Verification	
Employing organization:	Person contacted: Date verified:
Employment dates:	Last position held:
Name of supervisor:	Other positions held:
Basic duties and responsibilities:	
Description of performance:	Comparison with person currently performing the job:
Attendance:	Attitude:
Example of outstanding performance:	
Compensation upon departure:	Reason for leaving:
Eligible for promotion?	Eligible for rehire?
Reservations about hiring:	
Additional comments:	

Figure 10-1. Sample background check sheet

Getting Employment References to Cooperate

If only it were this simple. You know the old saying, "Ask and you shall receive"? Unfortunately, it doesn't always apply when it comes to checking references. In our highly litigious society, many employers find themselves in a double bind. On the one hand, as we learned above, you can be found guilty of negligent hiring if you do not show due diligence in conducting background checks. On the other hand, employers are increasingly concerned about disclosing information about former employees, for fear of being hit with lawsuits.

Past employees have successfully sued former employers for character defamation, when those employers gave unverifiable negative references. To win the case, the plaintiff must prove that the defamation was intentional. But fear of being dragged through the legal processes prevails.

As a result, many large companies have become wary about providing information. As a preventive measure, they've instituted policies of verifying only the most basic information (such as name, dates of employment, and last position held), regardless of past performance. This is extremely unfortunate, because often the best references come from past employers.

With the additional obstacle of having to deal with uncooperative former employers, you may be thinking, "Why bother trying?" Do not despair. Times may be changing. There are currently three elements working in your favor.

For one, organizations are beginning to realize they're part of a community. Consequently, companies are cooperating more often with other companies and releasing more reference information about job candidates. Realizing the value of good background checks, companies are slowly modifying their tight-lipped referral policies to a more strategic "scratch my back, I'll scratch yours" approach.

Second, state legislation has made it easier (i.e., safer) for them to do so. Many states have adopted or are considering legislation aimed at protecting companies that provide reference information in "good faith" to other companies. This is often referred to as *qualified privilege*.

The following conditions must exist to invoke qualified privilege:

- Information must be given in good faith, without malicious intent toward the candidate.
- Information can be substantiated or proven. Opinions and untruths are not covered and need to be avoided.
- Information given is limited to the inquiry. A reference cannot volunteer information that was not specifically requested by the prospective employer, particularly negative information.
- Information must be communicated to the proper parties, at the proper time, and through the proper methods.

The last point is the crux of qualified privilege. Reference information can be conveyed only in private conversations with individuals who have a legitimate need to know—usually only prospective employers and supervisors.

> **Key Term**
>
> **Qualified privilege** The right to convey information about a former employee's work history is protected against defamation suits if the information is conveyed in good faith to parties with a legitimate need to know.

It's important to remember that you need to provide references with an opportunity to disclose negative information about an applicant. There are two reasons for this:

- If you don't ask for it, you probably won't get it. For the legal reasons cited above, references will likely be unwilling to disclose negative information unless you ask for it.
- If litigation results, the plaintiff must prove intent. If a negative reference costs the candidate a job, the former employer is likely protected by qualified privilege if that negative reference came in the normal course of inquiry, in good faith, with no intent to harm the candidate's chances at employment.

If mutual interest and qualified privilege aren't enough to uncork stubborn references, then maybe the third element is. In defense of current employers, courts have found previous employers liable for the negligent acts of an individual who was once in their employ. In these cases, the current employer contacted the previous employer to investigate the candidate's background. However, the past employer refused to disclose certain information. If knowledge of that information would have possibly caused the current employer to not hire the candidate (and thus prevented the negligent act), then the previous employer is guilty of *negligent referral.* In other words, a former employer can be found negligent for not providing a prospective employer with important information about a candidate.

Now that you know what you may be up against as well as what may be working in your favor, let's review some guidelines for conducting reference checks.

1. **Contact only professional references.** Talk with people who know firsthand about the candidate's work, such as supervisors. Personal or character references are generally a waste of time.

2. **Develop a rapport with references.** This goes beyond just being nice. Try to establish a common ground. Chances are you're talking with another manager who's been in your shoes. Clarify your needs, and try to appeal to his or her common sense and feeling of professional obligation to help you.

3. **Empathize with the reference.** Let him or her know that you understand how tough it is to be a reference. You may want to share some of your difficult experiences as a reference. However, do not empathize too much; after all, you want something from him or her.

4. **Network with cooperative references.** When a reference is helpful, ask if there's anyone else who is familiar with the candidate's work. Do this with each reference. By casting a wider net, you're less likely to miss important information. Also, these sources may be less rehearsed and more candid.

5. **Contact more than one reference.** We recommend speaking with at least three to five references—especially in

cases that involve negative information—before making your decision.

6. **Don't give up.** If the human resources department stonewalls you, don't be afraid to call back. Persistence sometimes pays off, as you may end up talking to someone more cooperative.

7. **Do not limit yourself to the obvious references.** Peers, subordinates, and customers are all good sources of information. This is especially true if the candidate will have supervisory or customer service responsibilities. Often, working through conventional channels, especially HR personnel, is the least effective method for checking background information.

8. **Focus on verifiable, job-related information.** Not only are personal information and opinions not useful, they can lead to trouble if they influence your hiring decisions. Moreover, references generally feel safer and see greater value in discussing job-relevant information.

9. **Put the onus on the candidate.** Require references. Inform candidates that you cannot hire them until they provide a professional reference who is willing to talk with you. There is no law prohibiting this practice. Plus, candidates who are less motivated or who suspect their references would be less than flattering will usually withdraw. This also works for obtaining school transcripts.

10. **Have the applicant sign a waiver.** Sometimes a document requesting the release of information (positive or negative) may be enough to get references talking. Review this option with your legal counsel.

11. **Go with what you've got.** The reference may feel more comfortable answering questions about information provided by the applicant on his or her application and résumé or during the interview. Read statements from the candidate and ask if the reference agrees or not. Ask for clarification, if possible. Is his or her agreement enthusiastic or just lukewarm?

12. **Listen to what references** *don't* **say.** Hesitations or pur-
    posefully vague statements may tell you a lot. For exam-
    ple, if you ask why the candidate left and the reference
    replies hesitantly, "Well, I, uh, do not feel comfortable talk-
    ing about that," or if you request a description of the can-
    didate's performance and the reference answers vaguely,
    "When he was here, he did a decent job," then you've got
    something to explore in conversations with other refer-
    ences.

13. **Be vague or indirect.** Being less than straightforward can
    work to your advantage as well. For example, by saying
    that the person in question will need to go through training
    as a new hire, you may be implying that the candidate
    has already gotten the job. Then, the reference may be
    more likely to provide information concerning the person's
    training needs. This might be useful.

14. **Contact references yourself, or use a professional agency
    for this task.** References are more likely to talk with you,
    a fellow manager, than with an assistant. Also, you can
    ask any follow-up questions on the spot.

15. **Remind the reference of his or her responsibility.**
    Obviously we do not recommend starting with this tactic!
    However, if necessary, you may want to cite a few points
    about negligent referral and qualified privilege. You may
    coax an uncooperative reference to open up. If you try
    this tactic, be diplomatic. You don't want to scare or alien-
    ate any references.

Verifying Institutional Data

Sometimes problems in background checking arise in dealing
with institutions. It is particularly difficult to get information
from the military or from high schools.

High school records are often not stored electronically. It
doesn't help much, then, to know a graduate's name and
Social Security number. You also need to know the year of

Is It Sincere?

If a candidate gives you permission to talk with a *current* employer, we recommend caution in interpreting whatever that employer may say. If you get a bland or even negative report, is the employer just trying to avoid losing a star? If you get a glowing recommendation, maybe the current employer is just eager to unload a dud.

How can you know if the reference is sincere? You've just got to trust your instincts.

graduation (and, for women, as appropriate, their maiden name). A candidate with a GED may have received it from an institution other than the high school he or she attended.

Your best bet is to use an authorization waiver, such as the one shown in Figure 10-2. This should be a separate release from the one candidates may have signed as part of their application. Having it separate is important, because the background check form (Figure 10-3, page 168) asks candidates for graduation dates and dates of service (which could be used to determine age). This form should also ask candidates for any other names that they may have used in their educational experience and, for GEDs, the institution and the date. Without this, you may not be able to verify institutional information.

When Should You Do Background Checks?

The best time to check a candidate's background is after the final interview but before making a conditional job offer. There are several reasons why this time is appropriate:

- After your final interviews, your applicant pool will be smaller, consisting of only the most suitable candidates. This helps keep costs to a minimum.
- If you conduct a behavior-based interview, you'll be able to verify the situations that the applicant described for you. We recommend that you do this.
- Candidates whom you do not hire will not know why they

In connection with my application for employment with you, I understand that an investigative consumer report may be requested that will include information as to my character, work habits, academic records, performance and experience, along with reasons for termination of past employment from previous employers. Further, I understand that you may be requesting information concerning my worker's compensation claims, motor vehicle operation history, and criminal history from various state, private, and insurance sources along with any public records available. Workers' compensation information will be requested only in compliance with the Americans with Disabilities Act and/or any other applicable state laws.

I HEREBY AUTHORIZE, WITHOUT RESERVATION, ANY LAW ENFORCEMENT AGENCY, ADMINISTRATOR, STATE AGENCY, INSTITUTION, SCHOOL, OR UNIVERSITY (PUBLIC OR PRIVATE), INFORMATION SERVICE BUREAU, EMPLOYER OR INSURANCE COMPANY CONTACTED BY [name of company doing the background check], TO FURNISH THE ABOVE-MENTIONED INFORMATION.

I further acknowledge that a telephone facsimile (fax) or photographic copy shall be as valid as the original. This release includes all state and federal agencies. According to the Fair Credit Reporting Act, I am entitled to know if employment is denied because of information obtained by my prospective employer from a consumer reporting agency. If so, I will be so advised and be given the name of the agency or source of information.

I authorize the National Personnel Records Center, St. Louis, Mo., or other custodian of my military records to release to [name of company doing the background check] information or photocopies of my military personnel and related medical records.

Signature _____ Date _____

Figure 10-2. A sample release authorization waiver

lost out, whether because of the reference check or because of the interview. This helps protect the reference.

• Some states stipulate that the only valid reason for revoking a conditional job offer is if the candidate fails a drug or medical screen. Poor referrals are not reason enough.

APPLICANT INFORMATION (please print clearly)			
Last Name	First Name		Middle Name
Maiden Name	Any other name(s) used		
Home Address			

City	State	ZIP	County	From MM/Yr	To MM/Yr
Social Security Number			Date of birth*		
Driver's License Number			State driver's license issued in		
High School	City/State		Year graduated		Name on diploma
If GED received, in what state	Tested in what location		Date received		Name used
Previous addresses (to cover last 7 years)					

Address		City/State		ZIP	
County		From MM/Yr		To MM/Yr	
Address		City/State		ZIP	
County		From MM/Yr		To MM/Yr	
Address		City/State		ZIP	
County		From MM/Yr		To MM/Yr	
Branch of service			Service number		

*This information will not be used for the purpose of discrimination. The Federal Age Discrimination Act of 1967 prohibits discrimination on the basis of age with respect to individuals who are at least 40 but less than 65 years of age. The laws of many states prohibit discrimination on the basis of age.

Figure 10-3. Applicant information form

Should You Do It Yourself or Use an Agency?

Given all that's involved in conducting effective background reviews, it may make sense to use an agency. This practice has become increasingly common, as evidenced by the large number of such companies hawking their services on the Internet. The big advantage of using an agency is that you're paying professionals who can devote themselves to the work

Using an Agency

If you decide to use professionals, make sure that they do the job at least as well as you would do it yourself. Here are some suggestions.

- Find out what services are available, the turnaround time for each, and the fees.
- Make sure you know exactly what the fees include.
- Ask to see sample reports. Make sure they cover the job-relevant items that you need covered.
- If the report does not cover everything, tell them what you need. Expect to pay some fees for significant customization, but the service should include minor changes, such as modifying the reference interview questions.
- Get a list of their recent client companies. Then check their references! Remember: past performance predicts future performance. If things don't add up, keep looking.
- Ask to see any documents associated with their services. Most agencies will have a waiver for candidates to sign granting an outside agency permission to investigate their backgrounds.

and who have the experience and resources to handle the tasks involved—particularly complicated credit analyses and criminal record searches. As a result, they're often able to do more detailed and in-depth checks than you could do yourself.

However, make sure you choose a reputable agency. As the employing party, you may be held responsible for actions taken by the agency. Sometimes background-checking agencies provide information that's not job-relevant and that you cannot use legally—arrest records and other information protected by privacy laws. It's also prudent to verify negative referral information yourself before using it to screen out an applicant. Information of this type needs to be treated very carefully.

Of course, convenience carries a cost. The fees for outsourcing background checks will vary widely according to the scope and depth of the investigation, the job level, and the agency. Conducting a detailed investigation for a high-level job could run into thousands of dollars, while a simple background check (three-year job history, high school education, and one county criminal record search) for a general laborer position may cost only $50. If you ask the agency to go back five or ten years, rather than just three, this could double or triple some fees.

Another consideration is that agencies have standard things they check. Additional charges often apply for customizing items such as reference interview questions. Again, knowing what you really need to check will prepare you to deal with background-checking agencies, if you decide to go that route. It may also help reduce some of the costs. The costs may seem high at first, but keep in mind that by this point in the process you've reduced the applicant pool to only the best candidates. Given the return on investment, with the right agency this is money well spent.

How Do You Interpret, Use, and Store the Results?

How you interpret and use the information gained from background checks revolves around job relevancy, again. For example, learning that a candidate had several accidents operating a forklift on the last job but was otherwise a good employee may not concern you if the position to be filled doesn't involve driving a forklift. However, any falsification of information should be considered seriously, because it says something about a candidate's ethics.

When you develop the list of job-relevant factors to verify, select the knockout factors, the characteristics you consider necessary to be successful in the position. If you knock out a candidate from consideration, note the reason on the background check sheet. If you created an applicant tracking system as we discussed in Chapter 4, it's a good idea to record it there as well.

Store the information from the background check along with the candidate's application and assessment reports. Make sure these files are secure and that only people with a "need to know" (personnel and hiring managers) can access them.

Manager's Checklist for Chapter 10

❑ Background checks can help your company get the right people—and keep out the wrong ones.

❑ Inform all applicants up front that a background check will be required. They have the right to know what's expected of them, and any applicants who are unsure about a check can withdraw from consideration early in the process.

❑ Check references, credentials, and training needs only insofar as they are job-relevant. Develop a list of job-related items to include in the background check.

❑ Decide which items in your list of job-relevant factors will be knockout factors. Stick to these decisions.

❑ Develop a list of questions to use when checking professional references. Have your questions prepared when you contact them. Remember that references should not offer negative information unless you ask them.

❑ If you decide to use a background-checking agency, compare the agencies in terms of services and experience, then choose carefully. You may want to split the work: you can check the references (a good idea anyway) and the agency can do the criminal and/or credit checks.

❑ Set up a filing system for the information. This is confidential material. Treat it as such.

❑ Decide at which stage in the selection process to conduct the checks. Then run checks on all candidates still in contention at that stage.

Making Final Selection Decisions

Jill observed the debate over the two job candidates as if she were watching a tennis match.

"Kyle has better problem skills," Frank served up, "and he's much more adaptable."

"But adaptability doesn't mean squat without the technical skills," Diane shot back. "Jack has better technical skills."

"We can train technical skills," Frank backhanded. "Kyle is more conscientious and responsible than Jack."

"Maybe. But what about job fit?" Diane lobbed back. "Kyle admitted that he doesn't like to travel, but Jack does."

"Well, perhaps we should collect more data and meet again later," Stan interjected, trying to diffuse the situation.

Great. That's just what we need to do—waste more time with another meeting, Jill thought as she looked at the clock again. The meeting already had eaten up an hour and twenty minutes, and they were no closer to making a decision than when they started the great debate.

This happened every time they had to hire somebody. The four managers would gather and spend a lot of time and energy going over the final candidates. Jill didn't believe that these group meetings yielded better decisions; they just took longer.

What was happening here?

The managers were unprepared. Not only did they lack an effective process to make final selection decisions, but they also obviously had differing viewpoints on what the most critical competencies were. As a result, they wasted time.

Often, decisions about applicants earlier in the selection process are easier than the final decision, the choice of the hire. To make these critical final decisions, you need a system. And the system needs to be based on logical decision-making criteria. This chapter addresses the following issues:

- Making sound hiring decisions
- Notifying candidates

Making Sound Hiring Decisions

With any hiring decision, there are always unknowns—even with the most comprehensive selection system. Accuracy is not absolute. You cannot have perfect knowledge about how well a candidate will perform in a given situation. Therefore, when making hiring decisions, it's important to concentrate on what you know and try to ignore the rest as best you can.

There are four main things to keep in mind when making final selection decisions.

- Use a systematic approach.
- Keep decision makers to a minimum.
- Don't delay.
- Don't overselect.

Use a Systematic Approach

There are three general approaches to selection decisions.

The first is based on "gut instinct." This approach is most often used in cases when a company does not have top-notch assessment methods like the ones we've outlined in this book. After meeting with a candidate, a manager or a group of managers makes a gut decision based on very little knowledge. Research has shown that the decision may be right about 10% of the time—perhaps slightly more often if the managers are extremely good judges of character. Because we are passionate advocates of using comprehensive, valid selection systems, we strongly recommend that you avoid using this approach for making final hiring decisions.

The second approach is highly quantitative—the exact opposite of the gut instinct approach. This approach generally involves averaging numerical ratings. The advantage of this method is that it minimizes the mistakes commonly made with gut instinct, errors in judgment or personal biases. Research has demonstrated that this quantitative approach yields much more accurate decisions than qualitative methods. It all sounds pretty sterile and scientific, doesn't it? Well, aside from being boring, this approach ignores the valuable insights that managers can contribute to the decision-making process.

The third approach is a combination of the first two. While it relies most heavily on the quantifiable data from the assessment process, it does not discount the importance of managerial judgment. This approach can be called the "weighted" approach, because it allows hiring managers to give more weight to certain competencies and less weight to others, depending on how important they are to success on the job.

The strictly quantitative approach and the weighted approach are both acceptable. By "acceptable," we mean that they use a standardized evaluation system that is consistently applied to all candidates. However, we recommend the weighted approach because strictly quantitative methods tend to compensate for a candidate's weaknesses—even when those weaknesses may significantly impact job performance. Let's take a look at an example that illustrates this point.

An electronics sales and repair company has one opening for an electronics technician. Two candidates, Kyle and Jack, have made it to the final stage of the selection process. The hiring managers need to decide which candidate is more qualified for the job and make an offer by the end of the week. They've already assigned ratings in each of the competency areas, using a 5-point scale (1 is lowest and 5 is highest). They've determined that the average rating across all compe-

COMPETENCY	Kyle's Rating	Jack's Rating
Adaptability	5	3
Attention to Detail	3	3
Conscientiousness	4	3
Job-Fit Motivation	2	4
Problem Solving	4	3
Responsibility	4	3
Technical Skills	2	4
Overall Average Rating	3.43	3.29

Table 11-1. Ratings for competency areas

tency areas must be at least 3.00 to be considered acceptable.

Table 11-1 shows a summary of the candidates' ratings in each competency area, based on their performance in the assessment process.

With the strictly quantitative method, you simply look at each candidate's overall average rating and choose the one with the higher average. Both candidates have met the minimum standard for the overall average rating, but Kyle's average of 3.43 beats Jack's average of 3.29. Your decision has been made. Kyle is the superior candidate. But is he?

Look at Kyle's technical skills rating. It's just a 2! Common sense tells us that technical skills are probably very important for an electronics technician. What happened? Kyle's high scores in other areas compensated for his weakness in technical skills. However, will his ability to quickly adapt to changes really compensate for his poor technical skills?

This problem does not exist when you use a weighted approach. With this approach, the hiring manager determines which competencies are most critical to the position. This is where expert judgment supplements quantitative data. Let's look at how the matrix might be if the hiring manager chooses this approach for deciding whether to hire Kyle or Jack (Table 11-2).

Competency	Weight	Kyle's Ratings	Kyle's Weighted Ratings	Jack's Ratings	Jack's Weighted Ratings
Technical Skills	2	2	4	4	8
Job-Fit Motivation	1.5	2	3	4	6
Attention to Detail	1	3	3	3	3
Conscientiousness	1	4	4	3	3
Problem Solving	1	4	4	3	3
Responsibility	1	4	4	3	3
Adaptability	0.5	5	2.5	3	1.5
Overall Weighted Average			3.06		3.44

Table 11-2. Weighted ratings for competency areas

You'll notice that the hiring manager gave the highest weights to Technical Skills and Job-Fit Motivation and the lowest weight to Adaptability. Kyle's overall rating, using the weighted approach, is 3.06. This is derived by multiplying Kyle's competency ratings by the corresponding weights, summing the products (24.5), and dividing by the sum of the weights (8). Using the same procedure for Jack yields an overall rating of 3.44. Again, both candidates meet the minimum acceptable standard for the overall average. However, Jack is by far more qualified than Kyle. Because Kyle lacks the technical ability and the motivation to perform the job successfully, he is a less desirable candidate than Jack.

When making hiring decisions, it's important to apply a set standard to each candidate. It's not wise to merely compare candidates, for none of them may meet your minimum criteria. In the previous example, Kyle and Jack were compared with each other because they were competing for one opening. However, each had to meet the minimum acceptable standard for the average overall rating.

It's a good idea to set a minimum standard not only for the overall rating, but also for each competency area. In essence, these minimum standards become knockout factors. If a candidate scores below the minimum acceptable standard in any competency, he or she would be knocked out of the running, even if the overall average exceeded the minimum standard. This keeps your selection standards consistent and maintains the quality of your workforce, because you avoid hiring the "closest fit" rather than the "best fit." Remember: it's crucial to avoid hiring

> ### Set Your Standard
>
> Relying on a set standard for candidates will help you avoid the temptation to settle on a candidate. If your best candidate is not minimally qualified, try again! Reanalyze the data on the applicants in your hiring pool, recruit again, or hire a temporary if necessary. Don't make the mistake of hiring someone less than qualified. You will certainly regret it later—maybe for years.

an unsuitable candidate. You don't have to find the "ideal candidate," but he or she needs to be at least minimally qualified.

You may want to create a decision-making matrix like the one in Figure 11-1. This is a good way to present all of the information so that decision makers can discuss each candidate's strengths and weaknesses. When you're discussing the evaluations of candidates, keep in mind that candidates must meet the minimum acceptable standards.

Keep Decision Makers to a Minimum

Involve only those people who need to be involved. Why gather everyone on the staff to make a decision? Aside from the

Competency	Weight	Cand #1 Rating	Cand #2 Rating	Cand #3 Rating	Minimum Standard
Overall					

Figure 11-1. Decision-making matrix

inherent problems and waste of time and energy, not everyone needs or wants to have input. Moreover, since you'll be discussing candidate strengths and weaknesses (and possibly accommodations), there are confidentiality issues that may become important after a candidate is hired.

As a general rule, invite only those people who will be directly responsible for reviewing the candidate's job performance and those people who may need to interact with the new hire regularly, such as fellow team members or managers in other departments.

Be Purposeful

You can avoid losing a candidate due to delays by moving forward purposefully. Communicate the importance of selection decisions to everyone in your organization. Take them as seriously as you would any capital investment. Minimize delays by keeping scheduled meetings. And don't let those meetings suffer from "analysis paralysis." Focus on what you know and make a decision. The decision may be to collect more data before making a final decision. Just make it as quickly as possible, then act on it!

Don't Delay

The best candidates are hot commodities now, with the competition in the labor market. You certainly don't want to spend a lot of time making a decision, only to find out that the candidate you finally choose has accepted another job or isn't interested any more. Decide quickly—not in haste but quickly.

You can't delay hiring, hoping the sales price will drop, the way you can with other "capital purchases." If anything, the costs may increase if you find yourself in a bidding war for a top candidate or have to recruit all over again.

Don't Overselect

This advice is commonly ignored. After all, we typically want the best we can get in all things. We may be dazzled by someone who's overqualified. For example, you may be tempted to hire as your administrative assistant that extremely bright and personable candidate with a four-year college degree who sees the position as a stepping-stone to better positions within your company. That's OK—but you'd better communicate the position expectations very clearly or be prepared to replace that hire in six months!

We are not recommending that you settle for less than you need. We made that clear above. But, if you select candidates with developmental needs, you allow room for growth—within the position. Candidates who are overqualified may find the position not very challenging and become bored. This leads to dissatisfaction and turnover—just what good selection techniques should prevent.

How Should You Notify Candidates?

When notifying applicants about a hiring decision, you need to remember the three C's—consistency, courtesy, and candor.

Consistency

Treat every applicant with equal fairness. Do not notify some but not others. To avoid trouble, make sure you have a standard process and that everyone sticks to it. It's important to develop both a rejection process and an acceptance process. Often companies forsake one for the other. Oddly enough, it's often the acceptance process that gets neglected.

When making offers, we recommend that you first notify the candidate verbally. Negotiate an offer and reach an agreement. Afterward, it's a good idea to create a letter of confirmation (especially for all salary-level positions) that clearly documents the terms of the agreement.

> **CAUTION!**
>
> **Don't Be Too Specific**
>
> When creating agreement documents, make sure your language will not get you into trouble later. For example, quote *weekly* salaries and refer to *periodic* reviews, rather than *annual* salaries and *specific* review dates. This leaves you an out, if you should ever need it. Remember: nothing is permanent (or even long term), so do not imply that it is.

Include an "employment at will" statement, if possible, stating that employment can be terminated by either the employee or the employer at any time with or without cause.

Courtesy

Notify candidates as soon as possible: don't leave them waiting and wondering. Every applicant interviewed should be notified within ten days of the interview—even if you can say only that he or she is "on hold." After you make your hiring decision, notify all candidates immediately. Handle rejections with consideration for the

> ### Don't Reveal Reasons
> When communicating rejections, you do not need to reveal the reasons for your decision. We recommend avoiding any reference to the specific selection criteria.

candidates' feelings. When making offers, exude warmth and enthusiasm. (We'll cover offers in Chapter 12.)

Candor

Be honest and up-front. If you're not interested in a candidate, say so clearly. Don't allude to future employment possibilities if none really exist. Tell the truth. Most candidates appreciate a straight answer, so they can get closure and move on. Figure 11-2 on page 181 shows an example of a typical rejection letter.

Manager's Checklist for Chapter 11

❑ Hiring decisions require structured methodology and standard evaluation criteria that are applied consistently to all candidates.

❑ Use a weighted approach to make hiring decisions, so that you can assess competencies in relation to their importance to the job.

❑ Involve only those people needed to make a decision, generally those to whom the person will be responsible and those who will interact directly with the new employee.

Name
Street Address
City, State ZIP

Dear Applicant:

Thank you for your interest in the maintenance technician position
opportunities at Fuzzy Dice, Inc. We have reviewed your application, as
well as your performance in the assessment activities. A large number of
people have applied for the available positions. Each applicant is evaluated
against the same job-relevant requirements to ensure consistency and
fairness.

Our review of your performance and qualifications indicates that a good
fit does not presently exist for the position for which you applied.
Consequently, we are not able to offer you a position with Fuzzy Dice
and will not be moving your application forward in the selection process.

Thank you again for your interest. Best of luck in your future job search
activities.

Sincerely,

Hiring Manager
Fuzzy Dice, Inc.

Figure 11-2. A typical rejection letter

❑ Make your decision with all due expediency, as qualified
   candidates who are here today may be gone tomorrow.
❑ If you're considering an overqualified candidate, make sure
   the job is challenging enough so that you won't need to be
   recruiting for that position six months later.
❑ Send acceptance and rejection letters to all candidates in a
   timely fashion. Be consistent, courteous, and candid.

Offer and Orientation

Joe immediately stopped what he was doing when his assistant told him that Margie was on the phone. Joe had been anxiously awaiting Margie's call, after making her a job offer two days ago. Margie was a high-caliber, heavily recruited candidate. Joe felt fortunate to have found her. He'd already begun thinking about her start date and what projects he would have her work on first.

Joe was stunned when he heard why Margie had called. She was rejecting their job offer!

Speechless at first, Joe regained his composure enough to ask why she was rejecting the pay, benefits, and prestige that came with working for a Fortune 500 company. Margie explained that the pay and benefits were indeed better than with the other offer she'd received. However, she felt as if she fit in better at the other company. She could make an immediate impact there, and the career path looked brighter. That's where she belonged. There was no room for negotiation. She'd already accepted the other offer.

Joe was crushed—all that time and effort wasted. He sadly picked up his phone to tell his boss about the bad news.

What had happened?

Joe learned a hard lesson, that pay and benefits are not always foremost in a candidate's mind when considering a job offer. A lot of factors influence job decisions. For Margie, company culture and opportunities for growth were more important than pay and benefits. Joe had failed where the other company had succeeded—in appealing to Margie's needs.

This is the heart of this chapter. Once you've recruited and screened applicants and identified the ones you want, don't blow it by making a lousy offer or failing to show why your company is a great place to work.

In this chapter, you'll learn how to tip the scales in your favor the next time you want a highly marketable candidate to choose to work for you. Specifically, this chapter will address the following issues:

- Getting the ones you want
- Negotiating a win-win offer
- Orienting new employees

Landing the Ones You Want

This section outlines strategies you can use to attract and keep the candidates you're interested in hiring. Many candidates will accept your offer with little or no hesitation. But some will consider your offer more carefully, perhaps weighing it against other offers. This is where you need to concentrate.

Here are some tactics that can improve your chances.

1. Relax. Be friendly. Don't scare away your candidate. Make the situation as enjoyable and informative as possible. Focus on building a relationship. Remember: this is potentially the beginning of your working relationship.

2. Do whatever it takes. Your offer needs to be better than the others. You need to make an attractive offer and present it in a way that will catch the candidate's attention. You also need to be prepared to change your offer. Pay attention to the special needs of your candidate. Tailor your approach individually.

Hot Buttons

Offer something the candidate wants. Watch for "hot buttons"—what the candidate really likes. Play on them to attract the candidate and to keep him or her interested. If possible, anticipate candidate concerns early in the process. This is difficult, but it's worth the effort if you want to land the top candidates.

3. Be patient, but not too patient. Give the candidate time to decide, but be ready to act fast when necessary. Also, make sure you've exhausted all the possibilities before giving up and moving on. Patience may be a virtue, but so is the wisdom of accepting reality.

4. Don't be afraid to "sell" your offer to the candidate. At this point, the candidates have "sold" themselves to you. Now it's your turn to "sell" your company to them. Don't hesitate to ask, "What will it take to get you to come work for us?"

5. Don't play bait and switch. If you get a candidate interested in your offer, don't change it. For instance, if you offer two weeks' vacation, then change it to one in the first year of employment, you'll raise doubts and probably lose the candidate. Set reasonable expectations and play it straight.

6. Work for your candidate. This cannot be overstated. Once you've found the right person, proceed purposefully. Minimize delays and disruptions. Avoid rescheduling events such as interviews. Have a backup plan and resources in place to cover these plans. Share information early and often and keep the lines of communication open. This is particularly important concerning hiring schedules. If you plan on taking four weeks to make a decision, tell your candidates. If they cannot wait that long, it's better to know up

Treat Them Like Customers

Treat each candidate with care and importance. A good tactic is to treat them like customers. Ask questions to identify what they want and clarify misunderstandings. Strive to establish a common ground.

front, so you can concentrate on other candidates—or make a decision more quickly, if you really want them!

7. Don't hold out for "someone better." Sometimes it's tempting to pass up candidates who would be interested in the position while you hope and wait for a better candidate to come along. If the candidates in your pool are unacceptable, if they do not meet your minimum standards, then wait. But if the candidates meet your requirements, you should consider hiring them. "Someone better" may not come along—or he or she may not be interested in what you're offering. As a result, you may end up not hiring anybody.

8. Hold onto your hire. You want your candidate to thrive in the new position, so you need to deliver on what you offered and provide a healthy environment. Offer a "clean and green" work environment: it affects attitudes. Basically, make your company an enjoyable place to work. We'll talk more about this when we discuss orientation.

The most successful hiring managers are prepared and willing to change their methods, depending upon the conditions. If what you're offering isn't working,

> **⚠ CAUTION!**
> ### Don't Go Overboard
> It's important to lure your top candidates, but don't go overboard. Treat each candidate with fairness, respect, and patience. Present what you can offer and highlight the positives. Then give them some space and be available to answer any questions.

change it. If your presentation isn't luring candidates, change that too. And, if the labor pool is tight, you may have to be patient and concentrate on creating interest in your positions or try different tactics to expand the pool of applicants.

Hiring has gotten tougher and tougher, as the good candidates have more and more employment opportunities. Aside from pay, benefits such as

> ### Rejected Offers
> **Smart Managing**
> If more than a few candidates reject your offer, do a reality check! In their position, would you accept the offer?

Strategies to Get the One You Want

Here's a list of simple strategies that, for a small investment, often pay big dividends. These will help you gain an advantage over your competitors.

- Help with relocation plans (e.g., set up appointments with real estate agents).
- Help with finding health care providers.
- Offer fitness facilities or subsidized health club member-ships.
- Offer educational assistance or specialized training.
- Recognize special events (e.g., birthdays, weddings, births, employment anniversaries).
- Offer flextime, additional time off, or telecommuting options.
- Offer child-care options.
- Plan activities that involve employee families (e.g., organize an annual picnic at a local park).
- Have ticket or other prize giveaways (e.g., share those stadium boxes or balcony seats with employees).
- Host periodic luncheons or breakfasts (e.g., recognize efforts and celebrate successes).

health care and a 401(k) are now considered standard. Companies must focus on the other factors that candidates now find important. This is a complicated task, since people are interested not only in quality of work life but also in quality of life in general. Enjoying work is a very important factor for people today. They want good compensation and benefits, opportunities for advancement, and a motivating and challenging work environment. If you're not offering all of that, you'll lose candidates to companies that do.

Negotiating a Win-Win Offer

The first step to successful negotiation is to always be prepared. What do we mean by this? Well, when negotiating an offer, it pays to have as much information as possible, so you can avoid surprises. You do not want to put forth all that effort

recruiting and selecting candidates only to fail at the negotiation stage because you were unprepared. The following steps
will guide you toward achieving win-win negotiation outcomes
by preparing you to make an attractive yet reasonable offer.

Know the Market Value

First, find out the market value for any position you're filling.
Do not assume that whatever you're paying currently or paid
the last person in the position accurately reflects market
value. You can often get this information through the
Internet or from your
local economic develop-
ment office.

You may learn that
you're paying significantly over or under the fair
market value. If your
compensation is high,
you should have no prob-
lem negotiating an
acceptable offer with a
candidate. If you're pay-
ing less than market
value, you'll probably
need to do one or more
of three things: lower
your standards, raise your
offer, or sweeten the deal
with nonmonetary perks.

> ### Government Data—Free
> **Smart Managing**
>
> The U.S. Department of
> Labor conducts annual wage surveys
> for general positions types (e.g., com-
> puter operator and secretary). Local,
> regional, and statewide information is
> available and it's *free*. However, the
> reports will include a lot of informa-
> tion that you don't need, so be pre-
> pared to do some digging. Also, the
> data is not industry-specific, so you
> may need to supplement this data
> with other resources. For the most
> up-to-date and customized informa-
> tion, you should enlist the services of
> an expert to conduct a wage survey.

Know Your Limits

Once you know the current market value of candidates with
the skills you require, you need to know your negotiation
range. What are your financial limits? It literally pays to be
aware of how low or high you can go when negotiating an
offer with a candidate.

Money Isn't Everything

When we think of negotiation, we usually think of compensation. But the money is only one of your tools. Don't neglect other factors that make a job attractive. High-lighting these during a negotiation can get you further than you might expect.

Find Out What the Candidates Think They're Worth

A candidate may feel that his or her experience and expertise deserve more than the market average. Maybe that's true. Then you need to decide whether you're willing to pay more for the experience and expertise. If they're not worth it to you, move on.

On the other hand, a candidate may have lower compensation expectations than what you were prepared to pay. In this case, it's tempting to offer the lower amount and smile inwardly at the "deal" you got. Trust us: your new employee will find out sooner or later that he or she is being underpaid. Our recommendation is to fight this temptation. By offering more than a candidate is expecting, you succeed in thrilling him or her and in communicating your expectations. This way you create a desirable win-win situation.

Identify Who Has the Leverage

If you're having difficulty coming to terms with a candidate who's in demand, you need to identify who has the leverage— and quickly. In other words, who has the upper hand? Once you know this, you'll have a better idea of who needs to come to whom, so to speak. If there are other candidates in the pool who would be acceptable, then you have the upper hand. But if the candidate has the leverage, you need to nail it down and try to make it a nonfactor. Otherwise, you'll end up giving in or giving up.

Identify the Key Issues

Most negotiations center around specific issues or "sticking points." You need to identify what they are. If the issue is compensation (as it so often is), you need to adopt a negotiating strategy that will not end up costing you in the long run. For instance, offer incentives—both up-front and long-term—instead of raising the base salary.

> **Up-front incentives** Incentives that you provide before the new hire starts work—usually signing bonuses or relocation packages.
>
> **Long-term incentives** Incentives that you provide after the new hire has worked for your company for a specified period of time—usually performance-based bonuses or vesting programs that recur over time.

Some candidates may be enticed by *up-front* incentives. If you can afford them, they can cost you less than paying an inflated salary from year to year. However, we recommend *long-term* incentives. By tying incentives to performance, you lose nothing if the candidate fails to deliver what you expected. In addition, by tying incentives to tenure within a vesting program, you've protected yourself from losing money before you get a return on your investment. We jokingly refer to this as slapping the "golden handcuffs" on them. Candidates are less likely to leave if they have a long-term financial interest in staying.

Know When to Throw in the Towel

If you make several attempts but the candidate still rejects your offer, consider this. A candidate's rejection may be an indication that he or she is unsure about being able to do the job. Rather than admit to any doubts, a candidate may instead feign disinterest in the job or the job offer. You need to recognize this possibility. In such cases, trying to force a fit or to gain an acceptance will benefit neither party.

When negotiating a job offer, keep these points in mind:

- **Don't promise what you cannot deliver.** Remember: this may be the start of your working relationship. Be up-front and honest with the candidate. Provide a realistic job preview and clearly communicate your expectations and commitments.
- **Don't oversell or "give away the farm."** There are two main ways to oversell. First, you can offer too much in

terms of monetary and nonmonetary rewards. Second, you can take away too much in terms of the job responsibilities. Either way, overselling can result in a less motivated and less challenged employee. Another problem with overselling is that the employer might impose unrealistic expectations on the new employee, because the hire got such a great deal. Finally, other employees may be jealous of the new hire. In the long run, "giving away the farm" can hurt everyone involved.

* **Don't just wait.** If you make an offer and then don't hear from the candidate for two or three days, contact him or her. Ask if there are any questions or concerns that might be resolved. However, be careful. If the candidate is "playing games" (e.g., bouncing offers between companies), our advice is don't play. Ask yourself, "Is this the kind of person I want joining our team?"

Orienting New Employees

We've talked a lot about the impact of "first impressions" during the selection process. If the candidate becomes a new employee, you probably made a good impression. But what about the first impressions that new employees have when they show up to start their new job?

Too often, employers underestimate the importance of orientation. What happens in the first few days of employment has a significant impact on the big picture—on the attitudes new hires form about you and your company. This is your chance to impart key information, knowledge,

TRICKS OF THE TRADE

30/30

Develop a plan for the first 30 hours and the next 30 days. This is crucial. If you're unsure how to begin, solicit feedback from current employees, preferably those hired in the last 12 months. What would they have liked to have known from the start? Use this information to develop your orientation process. Then, use it consistently. Make it part of your company's routine, but don't let it be routine. Make it exciting—it's an opportunity to build enthusiasm!

and skills while the employee is most attentive and open.
Don't miss out on it!

"Sink or swim" orientation programs generally fail—particularly in large organizations—because they assume people will
eventually learn what they need to know on their own. That
may happen, but it still isn't fair—either to the new employee
or to the company. An effective orientation helps acclimate
the employee to the new surroundings. This takes time. Think
of orientation as a process, not just a day.

If you don't have a new employee orientation process,
start one. If you have one, think about how you might improve
it. Here are some ideas to get you started.

Day One

1. Be prepared. Have a schedule ready. Think about what the
new hire needs to know for his or her position. You should
have all the necessary materials and information already organized. For instance, if the employee needs safety equipment,
have it on hand and show how to properly use it. Think about
including a "gift," like a company pen, hat, or T-shirt. This
helps to build pride in the company.

2. Welcome the new employee. Greet him or her warmly. Try
not to appear hurried for time (even if you are!) by rushing
through a quick, insincere greeting. Assign someone to serve
as "tour guide"—someone with the time to give the new
employee the attention he or she deserves. Prepare a space to
sit down with the new employee. Show that you're excited that
he or she is joining the organization.

3. Take care of all the paperwork. Completing employment
forms and signing insurance documents is necessary and
sometimes forgotten, so get it out of the way as soon as possible. This leaves you time to concentrate on the "good stuff."

4. Overview important policies and procedures. That may not
be exciting stuff, but it's important. To avoid information over-
load, don't go into too much detail; just hit the high points.
You should also discuss work hours and when and how the
new hire will be paid.

5. Communicate the company vision or mission. Most organizations have a vision or mission statement. If so, refer to it. Don't just read it or give the employee a copy. Explain what it means, how it influences the company's decisions and day-to-day operations. And, most important, communicate how the new hire's role fits into and supports that vision. Try to stay focused on the big picture, as new employees are usually not yet ready to absorb details.

6. Clearly outline expectations. Explain to the new hire what he or she will be doing and what your expectations are. Do this for the first few days, the first few weeks, months, etc. New employees often feel confused, even lost. Establish periodic reviews to track progress and stick to them. Remember to empathize with the new hire—you were once in his or her shoes. Acknowledge how tough and confusing it is at first. Provide encouragement and support.

7. Provide a RJP. A good orientation will also provide new hires with a realistic job preview (RJP). There should be no real surprises here, if you provided a good RJP during the hiring process, but now the person can actually experience it. Be honest and up-front about the positive and potentially negative aspects of the position.

8. Take a tour. Whether you work in a large factory or a small office, show the new employee around. Introduce him or her to co-workers. Point out where he or she will be working and where to go for help. Use the tour as an opportunity to compliment and build up other employees by pointing out their strengths. For instance, consider this simple introduction: "Emma, this is Julie, our newest

Smart Managing

Make Them Feel Welcome

If possible, introduce the new hire to the top manager. This truly goes a long way toward making the person feel welcome. If that's not possible, then try to have the top person drop a note in the new hire's first paycheck welcoming him or her to the company. Small efforts often yield big rewards.

hire. Julie, if you need help fixing any machine here, Emma is the one to ask. She's one of our top technicians." This produces three benefits. One, Julie knows who can help with a problem. Two, Emma feels appreciated. Three, Julie sees that in your company managers appreciate the employees. Finally, don't forget to show the new employee where the rest rooms are!

9. Assign a buddy or a mentor. Remember that orientation is a long-term process. You cannot be there all the time, so assign someone to help guide the new hire through the first 30 days and possibly the first year. Mentors (or coaches) do more than orient new employees and build camaraderie; they also train and instruct them. Because they have a significant impact on shaping a new employee's initial impressions and actions, choose mentors carefully.

Here are some guidelines for selecting mentors:

- Select people who are doing the same job or a similar job or who will be interacting with the new employee frequently. There must be a common ground.
- Select people who are relatively new. Employees who have been there a long time may forget what it's like to be a new hire. Employees hired within the past 9 to 18 months generally can relate best to what the new employee is feeling and what he or she needs to know.
- Select people who have a positive attitude about the company and about their job. This is common sense: you're trying to build enthusiasm and commitment, not squelch it!
- Select people who are high performers or who are good at their job. A mentor needs to be a positive model. You want new employees to learn the right way to do things.

Being a mentor is a responsibility that should be taken seriously. Have you ever said something like, "I wish more of our employees were like Pete?" Well, here's your chance to help make that wish a reality. Ask Pete and others like him to serve as mentors. Make sure Pete is willing to do this and fully understands his responsibility. It helps if you make being a mentor a positive thing, something employees want to do. Give recognition to employees who volunteer to be mentors and offer incentives to employees who mentor effectively.

Beyond Day One

Once initial orientation is complete, don't stop. Employees tend to leave jobs because they're untrained and unmotivated. When they feel unfulfilled in their jobs, they tend to look for opportunities elsewhere. The following suggestions will help keep employees committed.

Orientation Is Not Probation

Do not confuse *orientation* with *probation*. Focus on helping the new employee become more comfortable with his or her work and the new work environment.

1. Keep the positive momentum going. Let employees know how important they are to the company. You can do this every day. A word of praise and encouragement takes only a few seconds but can do a lot to motivate employees to continue giving their best.

2. Provide ongoing training. You need to equip employees with the tools and knowledge they need to succeed. The success factors may change over time, so keep employees updated and informed.

3. Talk *with* (not just *to*) employees. Managers and employees need to have two-way communication regarding work performance, contribu-

Address Your Mistakes

If significant performance problems arise and it becomes clear that you've made a hiring mistake, be prepared to deal with it head on. Do not ignore the situation. You may have to move the new employee to another position—one better suited to his or her abilities. Or you may have to take documented steps to terminate the individual.

Unfortunately, assessment results just predict performance; they do not guarantee it.

tions, career paths, and future compensation. Career growth does not have to involve a promotion. Growth should occur within each position, as employees learn new skills and tasks.

4. Use effective feedback—early and often. As a starting point for feedback discussions, you can use the competency matrix that you developed to evaluate the candidates. However, don't be too critical of initial performance. We all need a period of adjustment. Be empathetic and encouraging.

5. Capitalize on the opportunity to learn from your new hires. What was successful? What was not? Do this through direct observation, asking for feedback from new hires and conducting quantitative analyses (such as validation studies). Evaluate your systems (from recruitment through orientation) on a regular basis and take steps to implement the needed changes.

Manager's Checklist for Chapter 12

❑ Each job offer will be different. The content of the offer may be the same for every candidate, but you should tailor the presentation to the needs of the individual.

❑ Be prepared when you negotiate. Gather all of the available information. Know what you have to offer and be prepared to sell it. Highlight the positives, especially those that put you ahead of your competitors.

❑ Negotiate for a win-win situation. Remember: this should be the start of your working relationship.

❑ Know when to pursue and when to give up.

❑ Start with a great orientation program, then keep it going. Praise, encouragement, ongoing training, two-way communication, and feedback help to keep employees committed.

❑ Remember: negotiations and orientation set the tone for future employee-employer relations.

Alternative Staffing Options

A large telecommunication manufacturing company outside Dallas was experiencing a mixed blessing. While sales of its products had greatly increased over the last three years, its ability to attract quality workers to keep up with customer demands was diminishing. The situation required immediate action, so the company decided to use an outside agency to fill some of the positions temporarily, until it could get its staffing strategy under control.

Things got off to a great start, as all vacancies were quickly filled. The human resources staff felt a sense of relief because now they were no longer responsible for filling open positions. It was so simple. They merely called the temporary agency and, within a few days, contract employees appeared. This situation seemed too good to be true. And it was.

After three years, the situation was chaotic. Turnover had skyrocketed and the workforce now was over 50% contract employees.

What happened?

The company took a Band-Aid approach to staffing problems, but never followed up with the cure. The HR staff never got around to fixing their staffing function. Nor did they develop a plan for most effectively using the agency to meet the company's long-term staffing needs. In essence, they got too much of a good thing and it turned bad. The company had mistaken *quantity* for *quality,* traded *recruitment* costs for *training* costs, and had become intoxicated with quick new hires, only to awaken each day to the painful hangover of low performance and high turnover. The company had lost control of its workforce, and its culture had changed to haunt it.

Using alternative staffing options can be a smart move for most companies—when done correctly. In this chapter, you'll learn about:

- Advantages of creating a blended workforce
- Alternative staffing options

Advantages of Creating a Blended Workforce

The flexible nature of today's companies requires a flexible workforce. Business needs are changing, and leading companies are prepared to fulfill these needs through various staffing alternatives. Full-time employees in permanent positions cannot keep up with the diverse demands. Many companies have found that a blended workforce provides the flexibility and expertise they need to keep their competitive edge.

> **Key Term**
> **Blended workforce** A workforce consisting of full-time, part-time, and temporary employees. This may also include contracting with individuals or organizations for certain functions.

Rather than spending a lot of time and money to recruit full-time permanent employees for positions that may not remain "permanent," companies are exploring the benefits of alternative staffing options. Such options can help break the "hire-fire" or layoff cycles that tend to damage the morale of the workers. However, the downside is that your full-time permanent employees may feel threatened by the use of alternative staffing options. And, employees hired through these options may feel like second-class citizens because they may receive lower pay and fewer benefits, and they may not truly feel like part of the team. Employers who choose alternative staffing options need to be sensitive to the needs and feelings of all of their employees.

Alternative Staffing Options

Almost every company can benefit from some type of alternative staffing. The key is to choose wisely and purposefully. Choosing *wisely* means that you should investigate all of your options and discuss how alternative staffing may impact your company and your employees. Choosing *purposefully* means that you should be proactive: alternative staffing should be viewed as a strategic move rather than a response to a desperate situation. Your staffing solutions should support your business goals.

Let's briefly review some of the more common options.

Part-Time Employees

Blending part-time staff with full-time staff is not a new concept. Permanent part-time staffing works well with certain positions, particularly those in which the workflow over time is steady, but not enough to keep someone busy 40 hours a week. There are also full-time jobs that can be shared by two part-time workers who alternate work-weeks. This type of arrangement often functions well with administrative positions.

Smart Managing

Part-Timers

If you have part-time positions that will likely remain part-time, look for candidates who really want part-time work—or you may experience turnover that can cost you in the long run. There are many people who want part-time jobs for the flexibility or extra income. Try to find these people. However, be careful not to let stereotypes influence your hiring decisions. For instance, do not assume that a woman with young children wants part-time work only.

Temporary Employees

The use of "temps" was historically viewed as a convenience—to fill in for

clerical and administra-
tive personnel who were
sick or on vacation.
Companies also used
temps for seasonal work
and really boring jobs
that had high turnover
rates. Today, employers
are realizing that tempo-
rary workers can fill a
variety of jobs, including
production and profes-
sional positions.

Do They Screen?

CAUTION!

Some temporary agen-
cies thoroughly assess
their employees—everything from
testing for job-related skills to conducting background checks. Others
do minimal screening. Keep in mind
that your company and a temporary
agency have different goals. A temporary agency tries to find people to fill
jobs. Your company wants to find the
right people.

The most common way to hire temporary workers is
through a temporary employment agency. An agency offers
several advantages to the employer:

- The temporary worker is an employee of the agency,
  which cuts down on your paperwork (e.g., tax forms).
- You do not provide benefits to the temporary worker.
- Temporary workers work when you need them—and only
  when you need them.
- Most temporary agencies offer temp-to-perm situations, so
  you can "test" how workers perform before you commit to
  hiring them.
- Many temporary agencies have screening tools to help
  match people and positions. This may save you the time
  and money that you would normally put into your selection
  process.

There are also some potential drawbacks to using temporary workers:

- Temps know that they will not be working anywhere for
  very long, so there's little incentive to cross-train or take
  the initiative to learn the ins and outs of the job.
- Because of the minimal lengths of stay and lack of benefits, temps may not feel much commitment to the organization and its mission.

Temps on the Internet

Smart Managing   Temporary staffing services are easy to find on the Internet. Use any search engine or directory to locate hundreds of staffing service providers. Your local yellow pages list such agencies under Employment Contractors/ Temporary Services. We advise that you exercise caution in your selection, because the quality and stability of these companies vary greatly, even among the largest ones, and even from location to location, within the same temporary agency. Ask questions. Make sure that the agency you choose can provide the type and extent of assistance you need.

- Trying to integrate temporary workers into a team environment is extremely difficult. Changes in personnel disrupt the team environment and reduce productivity.
- Turnover is high, as temporary employees generally seek full-time employment elsewhere.
- Often, temporary employees are working with an agency because they've been unable to secure full-time employment. This situation may reflect the quality of their work.
- Depending on the fit between skills and job requirements, training a new temp may take longer than you anticipate.
- Communication problems often exist. For example, in the South and Southwest, the first language of many temporary workers is Spanish, so companies must create bilingual communication systems.

You can also hire temporary employees directly, without going through an agency. In this case, you need to recruit, select, and do the paperwork, but this option also gives you more control over the workers.

Independent Contractors

The use of independent contractors involves contracting the services of an individual, for a clearly defined period of time, to perform a specific function or task. Contractors are usually individuals who can offer advice and expertise in particular areas. This could be a network specialist to create and manage your company's intranet or Web page, for example, or a process engineer to help you document your manufacturing process to meet ISO standards.

There are legal distinctions between independent contractors and temporary workers. A general rule of thumb is that if the individual is working only for your company, is using your installations and equipment (computer, telephone, fax, etc.) and reports directly to an employee of your company, he or she is more than likely a temporary employee rather than an independent contractor.

The major benefit of using independent contractors is that you get the expertise you need without retaining a full-time employee that you don't need. However, experts don't come cheap and remuneration policies may vary (e.g., by the hour, day, or project).

Use care and rigor in selecting your contractors. Choosing the wrong person can be a costly mistake. Often indepen-

---

Finding Temps on Your Own

Smart Managing

If you opt to find temporary employees without an agency, make sure you're clear about the duration of the job. Try to find people who truly want temporary work, especially if the job requires substantial training and a commitment for more than just a few weeks. Explore alternative labor pools. The American Association of Retired Persons, local physical rehabilitation hospitals, or college campuses may be great sources for temporary employees.

The Gray Areas

Mistake Proofing

Unless you don't mind having the IRS breathing down your neck, it's wise to consult a legal expert when using an independent contractor. Benefits and employment taxes for independent contractors are gray areas that need to be well defined ahead of time.

A legal contract for independent contractors should be written that outlines the duration of the relationship, roles and responsibilities, compensation for services, and the performance expectations.

dent contractors can be found via word of mouth. For certain positions, the yellow pages or the Internet may offer some guidance. Whatever method you use to recruit your candidates, be sure to get references.

Outsourcing

Outsourcing is becoming a popular alternative to hiring a full-time staff to perform functions that are outside of your core business functions. Outsourcing is basically contracting an outside company to perform functions in its area of expertise.

Outsourcing is not a new concept. Smaller businesses have always outsourced. For instance, the corner hardware store could not afford to hire a full-time accountant so it contracted with a local accountant. The small tool and die shop did not have its own trucks to move its goods, so it used a trucking company. Most manufacturing companies did not know how to get their products to the customers, so they relied on distributors.

Larger companies are traditionally more resistant to the concept of outsourcing. Opponents argue that it's best to do as much as possible in-house, that bringing outsiders into the picture may be a threat to the company's security and stability. However, more and more employers are recognizing that keeping everything in-house is less efficient. Simply put, they are wasting money. This is because there are specialized companies that can perform these tasks better and at a lower cost.

Today, many companies are realizing that their area of competitive expertise is limited. They are following the strate-

MISTAKE PROOFING

If You Outsource...

You will likely never even meet the people who are responsible for doing the jobs you're outsourcing. You need to be confident that the contracted company will maintain your quality standards. Investigate your options. Find out about the quality of its services, products, and workers. As with independent contractors, have a legal expert develop a written contract that defines the services to be provided and your performance expectations.

gy of focusing on their core business and looking at ways to get support from others in noncore areas. Outsourcing support activities such as accounting, advertising, or human resources selection is becoming a popular choice among many leading companies. The issues of security and stability are still there. The key is to outsource to companies you can trust and steer clear of the rest.

Manager's Checklist for Chapter 13

❏ Establishing and maintaining a blended workforce through the use of various alternative staffing options can work for many companies, but only if it's strategically planned.

❏ A blended workforce using part-time and temporary employees can provide you with the flexibility and expertise to expand your workforce when you need it and contract it when you don't.

❏ When considering any alternative staffing option, answer the following questions:
  • Why would this option be better than hiring full-time employees?
  • What business needs will this meet? What new problems will this create?
  • Is this option to be a short-term fix or a long-term business strategy?
  • How does this staffing alternative fit into our business plan?
  • What are the pros and cons?
  • How will we know if the option we chose is working?

❏ Monitor your alternative staffing to ensure that you maintain an optimally blended workforce. No single staffing option is inherently better than any other. The challenge is to find the right blend to maximize your productivity.

Index